JUMP Math 4.1

Book 4 Part 1 of 2

Contents

jump math™

MULTIPLYING POTENTIAL.

JUMP Math
One Yonge Street, Suite 1014
Toronto, Ontario M5E 1E5
Canada
www.jumpmath.org

Writers: Dr. Heather Betel, Dr. Anna Klebanov, Julie Lorinc
Editors: Megan Burns, Liane Tsui, Natalie Francis, Lindsay Karpenko, Daniel Polowin,
        Jackie Dulson, Dawn Hunter, Michelle MacAleese, Leanne Rancourt
Layout and Illustrations: Linh Lam, Fely Guinasao-Fernandes, Sawyer Paul, Ilyana Martinez
Cover Design: Blakeley Words+Pictures
Cover Photograph: © Phongphan/Shutterstock

ISBN 978-1-928134-91-6

Second printing June 2019

Printed and bound in Canada

Welcome to JUMP Math

Entering the world of JUMP Math means believing that every child has the capacity to be fully numerate and to love math. Founder and mathematician John Mighton has used this premise to develop his innovative teaching method. The resulting resources isolate and describe concepts so clearly and incrementally that everyone can understand them.

JUMP Math is comprised of Teacher Resources, Digital Lesson Slides, student Assessment & Practice Books, assessment tools, outreach programs, and professional development. All of this is presented on the JUMP Math website: **www.jumpmath.org**.

The Teacher Resource is available on the website for free use. Read the introduction to the Teacher Resource before you begin using these materials. This will ensure that you understand both the philosophy and the methodology of JUMP Math. The Assessment & Practice Books are designed for use by students, with adult guidance. Each student will have unique needs and it is important to provide the student with the appropriate support and encouragement as he or she works through the material.

Allow students to discover the concepts by themselves as much as possible. Mathematical discoveries can be made in small, incremental steps. The discovery of a new step is like untangling the parts of a puzzle. It is exciting and rewarding.

Students will need to answer the questions marked with a ▤ in a notebook. Grid paper notebooks should always be on hand for answering extra questions or when additional room for calculation is needed.

Contents

PART 2

Unit 8: Probability and Data Management: Graphs

Unit 9: Number Sense: Fractions

Unit 10: Number Sense: Decimals

Unit 11: Patterns and Algebra: Equations

Unit 12: Measurement: 2-D Shapes

Unit 13: Measurement: Time

Unit 14: Geometry: 3-D Shapes

Unit 15: Probability and Data Management: Probability

NS4-1 Skip Counting by 2s, 3s, 4s, and 5s

1. Skip count by 2s.

   a) 0, 2, 4, 6, _____, _____, _____, _____

   b) 34, 36, 38, _____, _____, _____, _____

   c) 1, 3, 5, _____, _____, _____, _____

   d) 27, 29, 31, _____, _____, _____, _____

2. Skip count by 3s.

   a) 0, 3, 6, 9, _____, _____, _____, _____

   b) 15, 18, 21, _____, _____, _____, _____

   c) 2, 5, 8, _____, _____, _____, _____

   d) 36, 39, 42, _____, _____, _____, _____

3. Skip count by 4s.

   a) 0, 4, 8, 12, _____, _____, _____, _____

   b) 50, 54, 58, _____, _____, _____, _____

   c) 1, 5, 9, _____, _____, _____, _____

   d) 47, 51, 55, _____, _____, _____, _____

4. Skip count by 5s.

   a) 0, 5, 10, 15, _____, _____, _____, _____

   b) 65, 70, 75, _____, _____, _____, _____

   c) 2, 7, 12, _____, _____, _____, _____

   d) 64, 69, 74, _____, _____, _____, _____

5. 52 shoes are in the front hall. 4 more people leave their shoes in the front hall. Use skip counting to find the total number of shoes.

   52, _____, _____, _____, _____

6. A tricycle, a bicycle, and a skateboard are parked beside each other. There are 9 wheels altogether. Four more tricycles parked beside the tricycle, bicycle, and skateboard. Use skip counting to find how many wheels there would be altogether.

 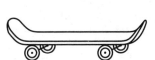

   9, _____, _____, _____, _____

NS4-2 Using Skip Counting to Estimate Large Quantities

1. Skip count by 10s.

   a) 0, 10, 20, 30, _____, _____, _____, _____   b) 35, 45, 55, _____, _____, _____, _____

   c) 450, 460, 470, _____, _____, _____, _____   d) 628, 638, 648, _____, _____, _____, _____

2. Skip count by 100s.

   a) 0, 100, 200, 300, _____, _____, _____, _____, _____, _____, _____, _____

   b) 1500, 1600, 1700, _____, _____, _____, _____, _____, _____, _____, _____

   c) 4790, 4890, 4990, _____, _____, _____, _____, _____, _____, _____, _____

3. Skip count by 1000s.

   a) 0, 1000, 2000, 3000, _____, _____, _____, _____

   b) 2300, 3300, 4300, _____, _____, _____, _____

   c) 3870, 4870, 5870, _____, _____, _____, _____

   d) 3329, 4329, 5329, _____, _____, _____, _____

You can estimate the number of dots in the picture by skip counting by 10s.

There are about four groups of 10 altogether.

So you can skip count by 10s to estimate there are about 10, 20, 30, 40 dots.

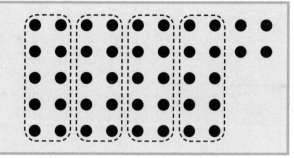

---

4. Circle other groups of 10. Estimate the number of squares in the picture.

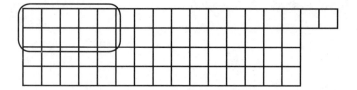

   The number of squares is about _____.

5. Ten jelly beans are shaded. Circle other groups of about 10 and then skip count to estimate the number of jelly beans in the jar.

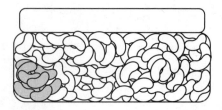

   The number of jelly beans is about _____.

100 dots are circled in the picture.

Sara circles four other groups of about 100 dots and then skip counts to estimate that the picture has about 100, 200, 300, 400, 500 dots.

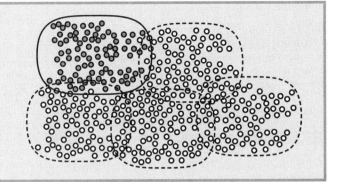

6. 100 sticks are circled. Circle other groups of about 100, and then skip count to estimate the number of sticks.

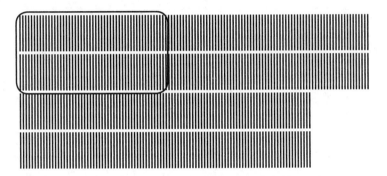

The number of sticks is about _____.

7. 100 stars are circled. Circle other groups of about 100, and then skip count to estimate the number of stars.

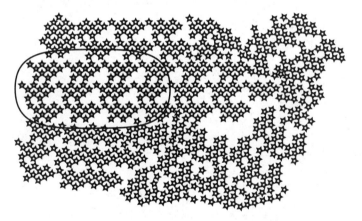

The number of stars is about _____.

8. Dory wants to estimate the number of people watching the football game in the stadium. She knows that every block of seats holds about 1000 people. She counts 7 blocks of seats that are completely full. One other block has a small number of people in the front row. Estimate how many people are in the stadium.

REMINDER ▶

4375

thousands | tens ones
hundreds

1. Write the place value of the underlined digit.

a) 35<u>6</u>4 _____tens_____

b) 1<u>3</u>36 _____

c) 25<u>6</u> _____

d) <u>1</u>230 _____

e) <u>3</u>859 _____

f) 2<u>3</u>8 _____

g) 6<u>2</u>14 _____

h) 8<u>7</u> _____

i) <u>9</u>430 _____

2. Write the place value of the digit 5 in the number. Hint: First underline the 5 in the number.

a) 5640 _____

b) 547 _____

c) 451 _____

d) 9050 _____

e) 1563 _____

f) 205 _____

3. Write the place value of the underlined digit.

a) 77<u>7</u>7 _____

b) <u>7</u>777 _____

c) 777<u>7</u> _____

You can also write numbers using a place value chart. Example:

This is the number 3264 in a place value chart:

Thousands	Hundreds	Tens	Ones
3	2	6	4

4. Write the number in the place value chart.

		Thousands	Hundreds	Tens	Ones
a)	5231	5	2	3	1
b)	8053				
c)	489				
d)	27				
e)	9104				
f)	4687				
g)	7060				
h)	760				

The number 2836 is a **4-digit number**.

The **digit** 2 stands for 2000—the **value** of the digit 2 is 2000.

The digit 8 stands for 800—the value of the digit 8 is 800.

The digit 3 stands for 30—the value of the digit 3 is 30.

The digit 6 stands for 6—the value of the digit 6 is 6.

5. Write the value of each digit.

a)
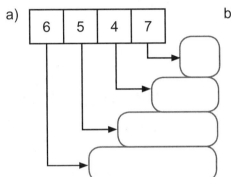

b)
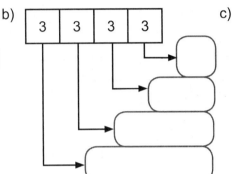

c)
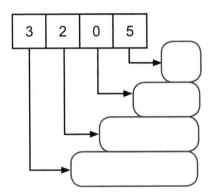

6. What does the digit 3 stand for in the number?

a) 237

30

b) 5235

c) 6382

d) 3280

e) 4305

f) 6732

g) 3092

h) 5883

i) 3852

j) 1003

k) 1300

l) 321

7. Fill in the blank.

a) In the number 6572, the digit 5 stands for _____.

b) In the number 4236, the digit 3 stands for _____.

c) In the number 2357, the digit 7 stands for _____.

d) In the number 8021, the value of the digit 8 is _____.

e) In the number 6539, the value of the digit 5 is _____.

f) In the number 3675, the value of the digit 7 is _____.

g) In the number 1023, the digit _____ is in the tens place.

h) In the number 1729, the digit _____ is in the hundreds place.

i) In the number 7253, the digit _____ is in the thousands place.

8. Write what each **1** stands for.

	Number	The First	The Second
a)	4121	*100*	*1*
b)	1312		
c)	2311		
d)	1501		
e)	7114		

9. The first number is worth how many times as much as the second number?

	First Number	Second Number	How Many Times as Much
a)	3000	30	*100*
b)	100	10	
c)	50	5	
d)	700	7	

10. Find the value of each bold digit. How many times as much as the second digit is the first digit worth?

	Number	Value of First Bold Digit	Value of Second Bold Digit	How Many Times as Much
a)	**4**1**4**2	*4000*	*40*	*100*
b)	7115			
c)	5828			
d)	9942			

NS4-4 Writing Numbers

Number Words for the Ones Place	Number Words for the Tens Place
zero one two three four five six seven eight nine	ten twenty thirty forty fifty sixty seventy eighty ninety

1. Write **numerals** for the number words.

    a) seven _____

    b) six _____

    c) eight _____

    d) twenty-three _____

    e) thirty-two _____

    f) ninety-five _____

    g) two hundred seventy _____

    h) four hundred seventy-nine _____

    i) nine thousand, two hundred seventeen _____

    j) five thousand, three hundred ninety-one _____

2. Write number words for the numerals.

    a) 1 _____ _____

    b) 7 _____

    c) 9 _____

    d) 6 _____

    e) 21 _____

    f) 67 _____

    g) 43 _____

    h) 55 _____

    i) 90 _____

    j) 13 _____

To write a number in the hundreds:

Step 1: Cover the tens and ones digits, then write the value of the hundreds digit.
Example: 743 becomes 7 ▨ and we write "seven hundred."

Step 2: Uncover the tens and ones digits, then write their value: "forty-three."
The number 743 is written "seven hundred forty-three."

---

3. Write the value of the hundreds digit.

    a) 342 _____

    b) 906 _____

    c) 891 _____

    d) 416 _____

4. Finish writing the number word.

    a) 207 two hundred *seven* _____

    b) 306 three hundred _____

    c) 804 eight hundred _____

    d) 590 five hundred _____

    e) 612 six hundred _____

    f) 872 eight hundred _____

5. Write number words for the numerals.

a) 118 _____

b) 320 _____

c) 835 _____

d) 385 _____

6. Finish writing the number word.

a) 7623   seven thousand, six hundred _____

b) 8432   eight thousand, four _____

c) 6127   six thousand, _____

d) 2417 _____ thousand, _____ hundred _____

e) 6501 _____ thousand, _____ hundred _____

f) 9840 _____ thousand, _____ hundred _____

g) 2054 _____ thousand, _____

BONUS ▶ 10 592   ten thousand, _____ hundred _____

7. Write the number word.

a) 6432 _____

b) 8854 _____

c) 787 _____

d) 3160 _____

e) 4900 _____

f) 5051 _____

g) 1060 _____

h) 601 _____

i) 1006 _____

8. Write the numbers words for the numerals on the signs.

a)

_____ Creek Park
(4)

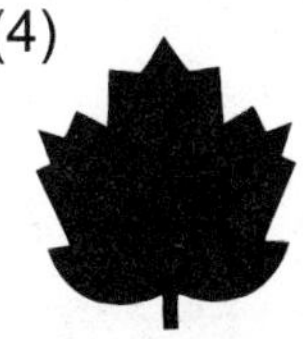

National Park

b)

House for Sale

(265)

_____

_____

Broadway Street

Inquire within.

c)

Score:

_____ points

(15)

d)

Come see the world's largest pumpkin!

_____

_____ kg

(681)

e)

Laptop for sale!

(650)

_____ GB

f)

(3625) _____

_____ **prizes available!**

g)

Mount Everest

(8848)

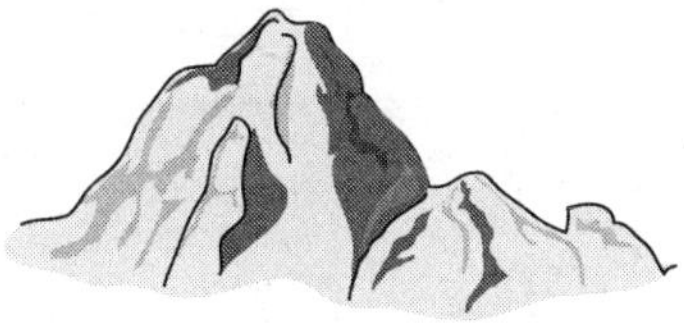

_____

_____ m high

NS4-5 Representation with Base Ten Blocks

1. Write the number in expanded form
   (numerals and words), then as a numeral.

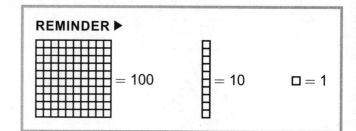
Example:

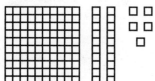

___1___ hundred + __2__ tens + __5__ ones = | 125 |

a)

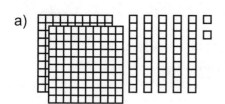

____ hundreds + ____ tens + ___ ones = [   ]

b)

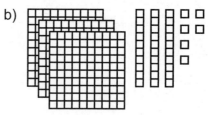

____ hundreds + ___ tens + ___ ones = [   ]

c)

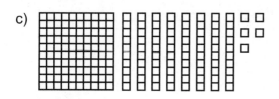

____ hundred + ____ tens + ___ ones = [   ]

d)

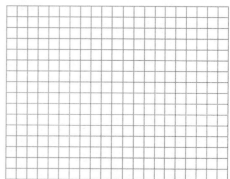

____ hundreds + ___ tens + ___ ones = [   ]

2. Draw a base ten model for the number.

Example: 123

132

3. Draw a base ten model for the number.

a) 68   b) 350   c) 249

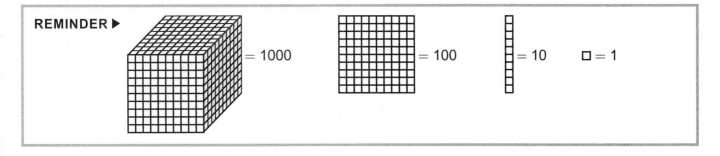

$= 1000$ $= 100$ $= 10$ $\square = 1$

4. Write the number in expanded form (numerals and words), then as a numeral.

Example:

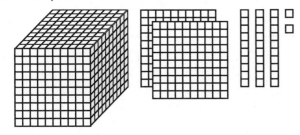

___1___ thousand + __2__ hundreds + __3__ tens + __2__ ones =   1232

a)

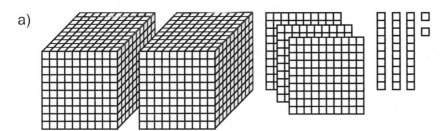

____ thousands + ____ hundreds + ____ tens + ____ ones = [   ]

b)

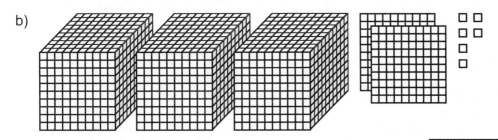

____ thousands + ____ hundreds + ____ tens + ____ ones = [   ]

c)

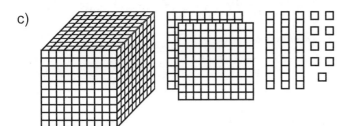

_____

NS4-6 Expanded Form

How to draw a thousands cube:

Step 1:
Draw a square.

Step 2:
Draw lines from three vertices.

Step 3:
Join the lines.

1. Represent the given number with base ten blocks in the place value chart.

	Number	Thousands	Hundreds	Tens	Ones
a)	2314				
b)	1245				
c)	3143				

2. Write the number for the given base ten blocks.

	Thousands	Hundreds	Tens	Ones	Number
a)					_____
b)					_____

3. Expand the number using numerals and words.

a) 2407 = __2__ thousands + __4__ hundreds + __0__ tens + __7__ ones

b) 4569 = ____ thousands + ____ hundreds + ____ tens + ____ ones

c) 3875 = _____

d) 7210 = _____ __

e) 623 = _____

4. Write the number in expanded form (using numerals).

a) 2613 = _____ 2000 + 600 + 10 + 3 _____   b) 27 = _____

c) 48 = _____   d) 1232 = _____

e) 6103 = _____   f) 5098 = _____

g) 3570 = _____   h) 2009 = _____

i) 903 = _____   j) 1010 = _____

5. Write the number for the sum.

a) 30 + 6 = _____   b) 50 + 2 = _____   c) 60 + 5 = _____

d) 400 + 60 + 8 = _____   e) 500 + 20 + 3 = _____   f) 200 + 50 + 3 = _____

g) 5000 + 700 + 20 + 1 = _____

h) 9000 + 600 + 40 + 5 = _____

BONUS ▶

i) 600 + 7 = _____   j) 900 + 6 = _____   k) 800 + 70 = _____

l) 5000 + 100 = _____   m) 5000 + 10 = _____   n) 5000 + 1 = _____

o) 8000 + 100 + 3   p) 7000 + 900 + 4   q) 4000 + 5

= _____   = _____   = _____

r) 6000 + 300 + 20   s) 8000 + 20   t) 3000 + 10

= _____   = _____   = _____

6. Find the missing numbers.

a) $200 + 70 +$ _____ $= 273$

b) $300 +$ _____ $+ 6 = 386$

c) $6000 + 800 +$ _____ $+ 7 = 6827$

d) $1000 + 400 +$ _____ $+ 5 = 1475$

e) _____ $+ 600 + 40 + 5 = 9645$

f) $3000 +$ _____ $= 3050$

BONUS ▶

g) $7000 + 200 +$ _____ $= 7202$

h) $6000 + 300 +$ _____ $= 6320$

i) _____ $+ 300 = 7300$

j) $6000 +$ _____ $= 6080$

k) $9000 +$ _____ $+$ _____ $= 9260$

l) $1000 +$ _____ $+$ _____ $= 1703$

m) $7000 +$ _____ $+$ _____ $= 7021$

n) $9000 +$ _____ $= 9008$

7. Write the number in expanded form. Then draw a base ten model. Example:

$3213 =$ _3000_ $+$ _200_ $+$ _10_ $+$ _3_

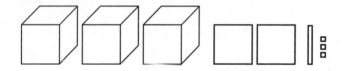

a) $2317 =$ _____ $+$ _____ $+$ _____ $+$ _____

b) $1446 =$ _____ $+$ _____ $+$ _____ $+$ _____

BONUS ▶

Jax has ...

- 1000 stamps from Canada
- 200 stamps from Portugal
- 30 stamps from Spain
- 9 stamps from Egypt

How many stamps does he have in total? _____

1. Write the number using numerals (in the box) and words (on the line below).
   Then circle the greater number in the pair.

   a) i) [____] [____] [____]   (268)   ii) [____] [____] [____]   [____]

   _____   _____

   b) i) [____] [____]   (____)   ii) [____] [____]   (____)

   _____   _____

   _____   _____

   c) Explain how you knew which number in part b) was greater.

   _____

   _____

2. Write the number in the box. Then circle the larger number in the pair.

   a) i) [____] [____]   (____)   ii) [____] [____]   (____)

   b) i) [____] [____]   (____)   ii) [____] [____]   (____)

3. Draw base ten models for the pair of numbers. Circle the larger number.

   a) four hundred sixteen   460   b) one thousand, three hundred   1007

4. Write the **value** of each digit. Then complete the sentence.

a)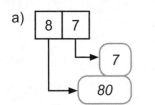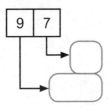

_____ is greater than _____

b)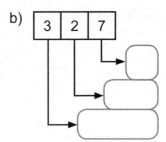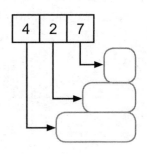

_____ is greater than _____

c)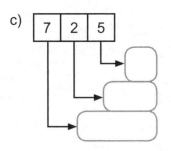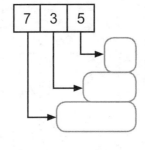

_____ is greater than _____

d)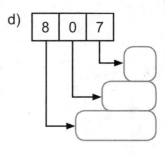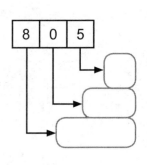

_____ is greater than _____

5. Circle the digits that are different in the pair of numbers. Then write the greater number in the box.

a) 24⃝7⃝5
   24⃝6⃝5

   | 2475 |

b) 1360
   1260

   | |

c) 4852
   4858

   | |

d) 6325
   7325

   | |

e) 384
   584

   | |

f) 2906
   2904

   | |

g) 875
   865

   | |

h) 238
   231

   | |

i) 3752
   3762

   | |

j) 3605
   2605

   | |

k) 9110
   9101

   | |

l) 3250
   2250

   | |

m) 8349
   8348

   | |

n) 9294
   9204

   | |

o) 323
   324

   | |

p) 5385
   6385

   | |

6. Read the numbers from left to right. Circle the first pair of digits you find that are different. Then write the greater number in the box.

a) 15⊘3
   15⊘7
   [ ]

b) 6293
   6542
   [ ]

c) 5769
   6034
   [ ]

d) 9432
   9431
   [ ]

e) 2847
   2874
   [ ]

f) 3207
   3270
   [ ]

g) 5986
   5988
   [ ]

h) 1492
   1483
   [ ]

7. Read the numbers from left to right. Underline the first pair of digits you find that are different. Then circle the greater number.

a) 23<u>4</u>2   (23<u>5</u>1)

b) 5201   5275

c) 6327   6102

d) 7851   7923

e) 7554   7550

f) 9236   8727

g) 3520   3502

h) 6683   6597

i) 2118   2148

8. Circle the greater number.

a) 2175   3603

b) 4221   5012

c) 6726   6591

d) 3728   3729

e) 8175   8123

f) 5923   6000

g) 387   389

h) 418   481

i) 2980   298

j) 8712   8912

k) 6439   6478

l) 7413   5412

m) 4819   5819

n) 5742   8742

o) 3456   4567

9. Write < (less than) or > (greater than) in the box to make the statement true.

a) 3275 [ ] 4325

b) 2132 [ ] 2131

c) 5214 [ ] 5216

d) 528 [ ] 3257

e) 7171 [ ] 7105

f) 287 [ ] 25

g) one thousand, one hundred six [ ] 2107

h) three thousand, four hundred three [ ] 3430

To find the greatest of three numbers:

Step 1: Underline the greater of the first two numbers.

48   41   73

Step 2: Compare the underlined number to the third number.

48   41   **73**

Step 3: Circle the greater of these two numbers.

48   41   (73)

1. Find the greatest of the three numbers.

a) 42   52   (53)

b) (274)   248   203

c) 616   827   519

d) 5872   3728   6278

e) 1057   1348   1903

f) 3070   3198   2185

g) 89   93   90

h) 522   418   367

i) 6134   5189   6143

j) 781   764   789

k) 3967   4982   4810

l) 8311   8131   9318

To arrange three numbers in descending order (from greatest to least):

Step 1: Find the greatest of the three numbers.

48   41   (73)

Step 2: Write the greatest number first.

___73___ , _____ , _____

Step 3: Write the greater of the other two numbers next.

___73___ , ___48___ , _____

Step 4: Write the least number last.

___73___ , ___48___ , ___41___

2. Arrange the three numbers in descending order.

a) 2628   2951   3455

_____ , _____ , _____

b) 5533   5630   5503

_____ , _____ , _____

c) 1077   984   1974

_____ , _____ , _____

d) 3402   340   4023

_____ , _____ , _____

e) 638   1638   863

_____ , _____ , _____

f) 4035   4953   5409

_____ , _____ , _____

BONUS ▶

g) 60 090   690   6900

_____ , _____ , _____

h) 7443   344 447   444 473

_____ , _____ , _____

i) 1 000 000   10 000   100 000

_____ , _____ , _____

3. Write a number in the blank so that the three numbers are arranged in descending order.

a) 87, _____, 80

_____, 87, 80

87, 80, _____

b) 642, 600, _____

642, _____, 600

_____, 642, 600

c) _____, 3860, 2608

3860, _____, 2608

3860, 2608, _____

d) 855, _____, 848

_____, 855, 848

855, 848, _____

e) 1001, _____, 999

1001, 999, _____

_____, 1001, 999

f) 4175, 4157, _____

4175, _____, 4157

_____, 4175, 4157

To find the least of three numbers:

Step 1: Underline the lesser of the first two numbers.　　　48　　**41**　　73

Step 2: Compare the underlined number with the third number.　　48　　**41**　　**73**

Step 3: Circle the lesser of these two numbers.　　48　　(41)　　73

---

4. Find the least of the three numbers.

a) (42)　52　53

b) 274　248　(203)

c) 616　827　519

d) 5872　3728　6278

e) 1057　1348　1903

f) 3070　3198　2185

g) 89　93　90

h) 522　418　367

i) 6134　5189　6143

j) 781　764　789

k) 3967　4982　4810

l) 8311　8131　9318

5. Arrange the three numbers in ascending order (from least to greatest). Start by finding the least number.

a) 2628　2951　3455

_____, _____, _____

b) 5533　5630　5503

_____, _____, _____

c) 1077　984　1974

_____, _____, _____

d) 3402　340　403

_____, _____, _____

e) 638　1638　863

_____, _____, _____

f) 4035　4953　5409

_____, _____, _____

6. Write a number in the blank so that the three numbers are arranged in ascending order.

a) 80, _____, 87

    80, 87, _____

    _____, 80, 87

b) _____, 600, 642

    600, _____, 642

    600, 642, _____

c) 2608, 3860, _____

    2608, _____, 3860

    _____, 2608, 3860

d) 848, _____, 855

    848, 855, _____

    _____, 848, 855

e) 999, _____, 1001

    _____, 999, 1001

    999, 1001, _____

f) _____, 4157, 4175

    4157, _____, 4175

    4157, 4175, _____

7. Mark the numbers on the number line. Then write the numbers in ascending order.
(Marks on the number line do not have to be exact.)

200   250   300   350   400   450   500   550   600   650   700

a) Use ● to mark 274, 248, 213.   _213_ , _248_ , _274_

b) Use ■ to mark 419, 449, 389.   _____ , _____ , _____

c) Use ▲ to mark 519, 616, 657.   _____ , _____ , _____

8. Mark the numbers on the number line. Then write the numbers in ascending order.
(Marks on the number line do not have to be exact.)

1000   1100   1200   1300   1400   1500   1600   1700   1800   1900   2000

a) Use ● to mark 1050, 1200, 1150.   _____ , _____ , _____

b) Use ■ to mark 1500, 1380, 1400.   _____ , _____ , _____

c) Use ▲ to mark 1840, 1700, 1960.   _____ , _____ , _____

9. Mark the numbers on the number line. Then write the numbers in ascending order.
(Marks on the number line do not have to be exact.)

8900   9000   9100   9200   9300   9400   9500   9600   9700   9800   9900

a) Use ● to mark 8990, 9800, 9090.   _____ , _____ , _____

b) Use ■ to mark 9810, 9100, 8910.   _____ , _____ , _____

c) Use ▲ to mark 9000, 8900, 9890.   _____ , _____ , _____

NS4-9 Rounding on a Number Line

1. Draw an arrow to show whether the circled number is closer to 0 or 10.

a)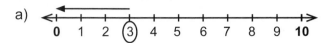

b)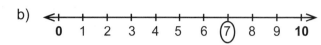

c)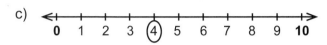

d)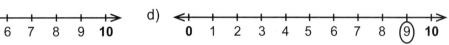

2. a) Which one-digit numbers are closer to 0? _____

   b) Which one-digit numbers are closer to 10? _____

   c) Why is 5 a special case? _____

3. Draw an arrow to show if you would round to 10 or 20 or 30.

a)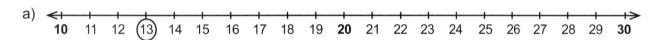

b)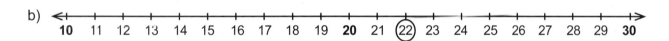

c)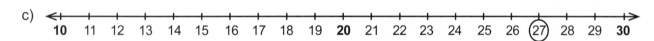

4. Draw an arrow to show which multiple of 10 the number in the circle is closest to.

a)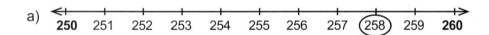

b)

5. Circle the correct answer. Use the number lines in Questions 3 and 4 to help.

   a) 27 is closer to: 20 or 30

   b) 24 is closer to: 20 or 30

   c) 19 is closer to: 10 or 20

   d) 13 is closer to: 10 or 20

   e) 26 is closer to: 20 or 30

   f) 12 is closer to: 10 or 20

   g) 251 is closer to: 250 or 260

   h) 258 is closer to: 250 or 260

   i) 333 is closer to: 330 or 340

   j) 339 is closer to: 330 or 340

6. Draw an arrow to the nearest ten, then round each number to the nearest ten.

a)

| 10 | 11 | 12 | (13) | 14 | 15 | 16 | (17) | 18 | 19 | 20 | 21 | 22 | 23 | 24 | 25 | 26 | 27 | 28 | (29) | 30 |

Round to: _____   _____   _____

b)

| 40 | 41 | 42 | 43 | (44) | 45 | 46 | 47 | 48 | 49 | 50 | 51 | 52 | (53) | 54 | 55 | 56 | 57 | (58) | 59 | 60 |

Round to: _____   _____   _____

c)

| 60 | 61 | 62 | 63 | 64 | 65 | 66 | 67 | (68) | 69 | 70 | (71) | 72 | 73 | 74 | 75 | 76 | (77) | 78 | 79 | 80 |

Round to: _____   _____   _____

d)

| 250 | 251 | 252 | (253) | 254 | 255 | 256 | 257 | 258 | 259 | 260 | 261 | 262 | 263 | (264) | 265 | (266) | 267 | 268 | 269 | 270 |

Round to: _____   _____ _____

e)

| 330 | 331 | 332 | (333) | 334 | 335 | 336 | 337 | 338 | 339 | 340 | 341 | 342 | 343 | (344) | 345 | (346) | 347 | 348 | 349 | 350 |

Round to: _____   _____ _____

7. Circle the correct answer. Then round the number to the nearest ten.

a) 27 is closer to 20 or (30).
   Round to ___30___ .

b) 16 is closer to 10 or 20.
   Round to _____ .

c) 39 is closer to 30 or 40.
   Round to _____ .

d) 31 is closer to 30 or 40.
   Round to _____ .

e) 62 is closer to 60 or 70.
   Round to _____ .

f) 251 is closer to 250 or 260.
   Round to _____ .

g) 348 is closer to 340 or 350.
   Round to _____ .

h) 258 is closer to 250 or 260.
   Round to _____ .

i) 341 is closer to 340 or 350.
   Round to _____ .

j) 256 is closer to 250 or 260.
   Round to _____ .

8. Draw an arrow to show whether the circled number is closer to 0 or 100.

a)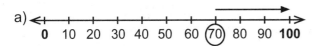

b)

c)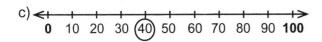

d)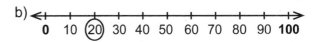

9. Is 50 closer to 0 or to 100? Why is 50 a special case?

_____

10. Would you round to 0 or 100?

a) Round 80 to: 0 or 100   b) Round 40 to: 0 or 100

c) Round 10 to: 0 or 100   d) Round 60 to: 0 or 100

11. Draw an arrow to show which hundred you would round to.

a)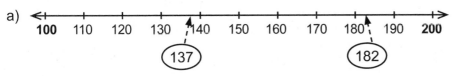

Round to: _____   _____

b)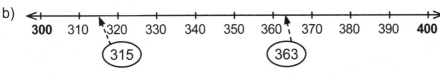

Round to: _____   _____

12. Circle the correct answer.

a) 153 is closer to: 100 or 200   b) 189 is closer to: 100 or 200

c) 117 is closer to: 100 or 200   d) 135 is closer to: 100 or 200

e) 370 is closer to: 300 or 400   f) 332 is closer to: 300 or 400

BONUS ▶

Show the approximate position of each number on the line. What hundred would you round to?

<+|—+—+—+—+—+—+—+—+—+—+—+—+—+—+—+—+—+—+—+|+>
500 510 520 530 540 550 560 570 580 590 **600** 610 620 630 640 650 660 670 680 690 **700**

(516)

a) 516   b) 576   c) 687   d) 629

Round to: _____   Round to: _____   Round to: _____   Round to: _____

13. Draw an arrow to show whether the circled number is closer to 0 or 1000.

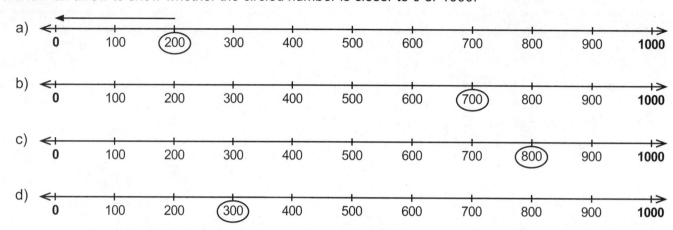

a)
b)
c)
d)

14. Is 500 closer to 0 or 1000? Why is 500 a special case?

_____

15. Circle the correct answer.

a) 100 is closer to: 0 or 1000

b) 900 is closer to: 0 or 1000

c) 600 is closer to: 0 or 1000

d) 400 is closer to: 0 or 1000

16. Draw an arrow to show which thousand you would round to.

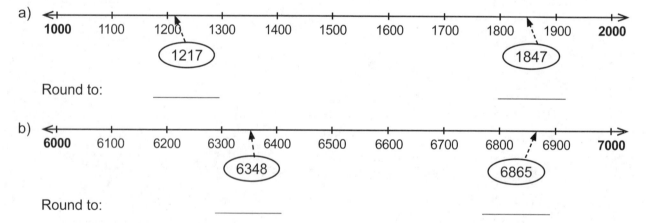

a)

Round to: _____   _____

b)

Round to: _____   _____

17. Circle the correct answer.

a) 1953 is closer to: 1000 or 2000

b) 3487 is closer to: 3000 or 4000

c) 6293 is closer to: 6000 or 7000

d) 8612 is closer to: 8000 or 9000

e) 5521 is closer to: 5000 or 6000

f) 3190 is closer to: 3000 or 4000

18. Write a rule for rounding a four-digit number to the nearest thousand.

NS4-10 Rounding

To round to the nearest ten, look at the ones digit.

0, 1, 2, 3, or 4—you round down
5, 6, 7, 8, or 9—you round up

1. Round to the nearest ten.

a) 16 [ ]   b) 23 [ ]   c) 72 [ ]

d) 66 [ ]   e) 81 [ ]   f) 93 [ ]

g) 14 [ ]   h) 59 [ ]   i) 65 [ ]

2. Round to the nearest ten. Underline the tens digit first. Then put your pencil on the digit to the right (the ones digit). This digit tells you whether to round up or down.

a) 14̲5 [150]   b) 172 [ ]   c) 320 [ ]

d) 255 [ ]   e) 784 [ ]   f) 667 [ ]

g) 441 [ ]   h) 939 [ ]   i) 316 [ ]

j) 520 [ ]   k) 985 [ ]   l) 534 [ ]

m) 758 [ ]   n) 845 [ ]   o) 293 [ ]

To round to the nearest hundred, look at the tens digit.

0, 1, 2, 3, or 4—you round down
5, 6, 7, 8, or 9—you round up

Example: 345. The 4 tells you to round down, so round 345 to 300.

3. Round to the nearest hundred. Underline the hundreds digit first.
Then put your pencil on the digit to the right (the tens digit).

a) 3̲40 [300]   b) 650 [ ]   c) 170 [ ]

d) 240 [ ]   e) 710 [ ]   f) 580 [ ]

g) 880 [ ]   h) 930 [ ]   i) 750 [ ]

j) 290 [ ]   k) 158 [ ]   l) 338 [ ]

m) 411 [ ]   n) 658 [ ]   o) 149 [ ]

p) 291 [ ]   q) 372 [ ]   r) 868 [ ]

s) 207 [ ]   t) 525 [ ]   u) 459 [ ]

To round 2531 to the nearest hundred, underline the hundreds digit: 2531

Then look at the tens digit. The 3 tells you to round down: 2500

4. Round to the nearest hundred. Underline the hundreds digit first.
    Then put your pencil on the digit to the right (the tens digit).

a) 2156 | 2200 | b) 4389 [   ]   c) 3229 [   ]

d) 1905 [   ]   e) 5251 [   ]   f) 9127 [   ]

g) 6472 [   ]   h) 8783 [   ]   i) 7255 [   ]

j) 1098 [   ]   k) 3886 [   ]   l) 4624 [   ]

m) 8077 [   ]   n) 6382 [   ]   o) 9561 [   ]

p) 2612 [   ]   q) 5924 [   ]

BONUS ▶

r) 2963 [   ]   s) 997 [   ]   t) 3982 [   ]

To round to the nearest thousand, look at the hundreds digit.

    0, 1, 2, 3, or 4—you round down
    5, 6, 7, 8, or 9—you round up

Example: 7826. The 8 tells you to round up, so round 7826 to 8000.

5. Round to the nearest thousand. Underline the thousands digit first.
    Then put your pencil on the digit to the right (the hundreds digit).

a) 2757 | 3000 | b) 9052 [   ]   c) 6831 [   ]

d) 3480 [   ]   e) 5543 [   ]   f) 4740 [   ]

g) 8193 [   ]   h) 2607 [   ]   i) 6107 [   ]

j) 9125 [   ]   k) 5114 [   ]   l) 7649 [   ]

m) 1336 [   ]   n) 8538 [   ]   o) 4226 [   ]

p) 7311 [   ]   q) 2864 [   ]   r) 3575 [   ]

s) 7992 [   ]   t) 9034 [   ]   u) 6481 [   ]

NS4-11 Regrouping

Carl has 5 tens blocks and 17 ones blocks. He regroups 10 ones blocks as 1 tens block.

5 tens + 17 ones   =   6 tens + 7 ones

1. Regroup 10 ones as 1 ten.

a)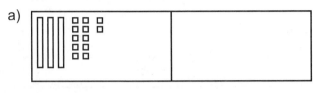

____ tens + ____ ones = ____ tens + ____ ones

b)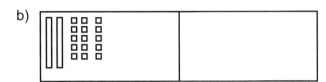

____ tens + ____ ones = ____ tens + ____ ones

c)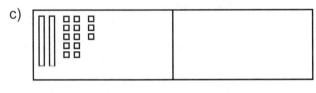

____ tens + ____ ones = ____ tens + ____ ones

d)

____ tens + ____ ones = ____ tens + ____ ones

2. How many ones can you regroup as tens? Complete the table.

a)
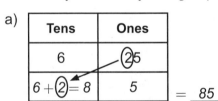

Tens	Ones
6	②5
6 + ② = 8	5

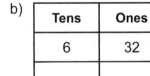 = _85_

b)

Tens	Ones
6	32

= _____

c)

Tens	Ones
5	31

= _____

d)

Tens	Ones
7	17

= _____

e)

Tens	Ones
6	29

= _____

f)

Tens	Ones
1	52

= _____

3. Regroup ones as tens.

a) 23 ones = ____ tens + ____ ones

b) 56 ones = ____ tens + ____ ones

c) 86 ones = ____ tens + ____ ones

d) 58 ones = ____ tens + ____ ones

e) 18 ones = ____ ten + ____ ones

f) 72 ones = ____ tens + ____ ones

g) 80 ones = ____ tens + ____ ones

h) 7 ones = ____ tens + ____ ones

i) 98 ones = ____ tens + ____ ones

Tristan has 2 hundreds blocks, 15 tens blocks, and 6 ones blocks. He regroups 10 tens blocks as 1 hundreds block.

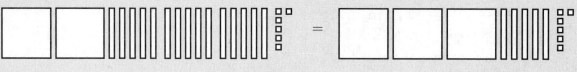

2 hundreds + 15 tens + 6 ones   3 hundreds + 5 tens + 6 ones

4. Complete the table by regrouping 10 tens as 1 hundred.

a)
Hundreds	Tens
5	(1)1
5 + (1) = 6	1

b)
Hundreds	Tens
2	15

c)
Hundreds	Tens
6	17

d)
Hundreds	Tens
6	12

e)
Hundreds	Tens
2	17

f)
Hundreds	Tens
5	10

5. Choose a table from Question 4 and model your answer using blocks.

6. Regroup as many tens as hundreds as you can.
   Remember: 10 tens = 1 hundred, 20 tens = 2 hundreds, 30 tens = 3 hundreds, and so on.

   a) 3 hundreds + 13 tens + 4 ones = _____ hundreds + _____ tens + _____ ones

   b) 5 hundreds + 21 tens + 1 one = _____ hundreds + _____ ten + _____ one

   c) 3 hundreds + 10 tens + 5 ones = _____

   d) 1 hundred + 34 tens + 7 ones = _____

7. Regroup tens as hundreds or ones as tens.

   a) 4 hundreds + 2 tens + 19 ones = _____*4 hundreds + 3 tens + 9 ones*_____

   b) 7 hundreds + 25 tens + 2 ones = _____

   c) 2 hundreds + 43 tens + 6 ones = _____

   d) 7 hundreds + 1 ten + 61 ones = _____

   e) 0 hundreds + 26 tens + 3 ones = _____

Mandy has 1 thousands block, 11 hundreds blocks, 1 tens block, and 2 ones blocks.
She regroups 10 hundreds blocks as 1 thousands block.

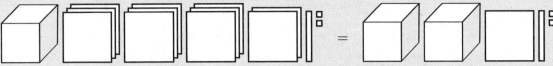

1 thousand + 11 hundreds + 1 ten + 2 ones   2 thousands + 1 hundred + 1 ten + 2 ones

8. Complete the table by regrouping 10 hundreds as 1 thousand.

a)

Thousands	Hundreds
3	12
3 + 1 = 4	2

b)

Thousands	Hundreds
4	13

c)

Thousands	Hundreds
7	14

9. Choose a table from Question 8 and model your answer using blocks.

10. Regroup hundreds as thousands, tens as hundreds, or ones as tens.

a) 5 thousands + 12 hundreds + 3 tens + 1 one

   = ___6___ thousands + ___2___ hundreds + ___3___ tens + ___1___ one

b) 3 thousands + 15 hundreds + 1 ten + 6 ones

   = _____ thousands + _____ hundreds + _____ ten + _____ ones

c) 3 thousands + 26 hundreds + 5 tens + 1 one

   = _____ thousands + _____ hundreds + _____ tens + _____ one

d) 6 thousands + 6 hundreds + 23 tens + 5 ones

   = _____

e) 6 thousands + 14 hundreds + 7 tens + 25 ones

   = _____

11. Raj wants to build a model of the number three thousand, two hundred twelve.

   He has 3 thousands blocks, 1 hundreds block, and 24 ones blocks.

   Can he build the model?

   Use diagrams and numbers to justify your answer.

1. Add the numbers by drawing a picture and adding the digits.

a) $15 + 43$

	With base ten blocks		With numerals	
	Tens	Ones	Tens	Ones
15	▮	□□□□□	1	5
43	▮▮▮▮	□□□	4	3
sum	▮▮▮▮▮	□□□□□ □□□	5	8

$15 + 43 =$ _____

b) $25 + 22$

	With base ten blocks		With numerals	
	Tens	Ones	Tens	Ones
25				
22				
sum				

$25 + 22 =$ _____

c) $31 + 27$

	With base ten blocks		With numerals	
	Tens	Ones	Tens	Ones
31				
27				
sum				

$31 + 27 =$ _____

d) $13 + 24$

	With base ten blocks		With numerals	
	Tens	Ones	Tens	Ones
13				
24				
sum				

$13 + 24 =$ _____

2. Add the numbers by adding the digits.

a)
```
   3  4
+  4  3
_____
```

b)
```
   7  7
+  1  2
_____
```

c)
```
   5  4
+  3  5
_____
```

d)
```
   1  0
+  4  9
_____
```

e)
```
   1  6
+  2  3
_____
```

f)
```
   1  6
+  2  1
_____
```

g)
```
   5  2
+  2  4
_____
```

h)
```
   8  1
+  1  1
_____
```

i)
```
   4  3
+  3  1
_____
```

j)
```
   7  5
+  1  4
_____
```

NS4-13 Adding 2-Digit Numbers (Regrouping)

1. Add the numbers by drawing a picture and adding the digits.
   Regroup to find the sum.

a) 16 + 25

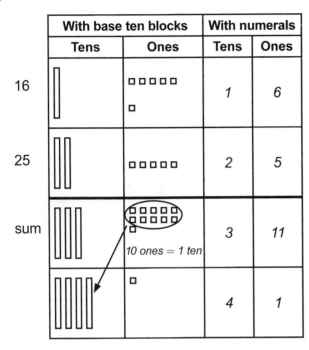

	With base ten blocks		With numerals	
	Tens	Ones	Tens	Ones
16			1	6
25			2	5
sum		10 ones = 1 ten	3	11
			4	1

16 + 25 = ___41___

b) 25 + 37

	With base ten blocks		With numerals	
	Tens	Ones	Tens	Ones
25				
37				
sum				

25 + 37 = _____

c) 29 + 36

	With base ten blocks		With numerals	
	Tens	Ones	Tens	Ones
29				
36				
sum				

29 + 36 = _____

d) 18 + 35

	With base ten blocks		With numerals	
	Tens	Ones	Tens	Ones
18				
35				
sum				

18 + 35 = _____

2. Add the numbers with regrouping.

Step 1: Add the numbers in the ones column. Regroup 10 ones as 1 ten.

tens go here

a)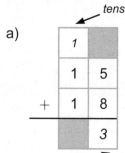
```
  1
  1 5
+ 1 8
    3
```
ones go here

b)
```
  6 4
+ 1 6
```

c)
```
  7 5
+ 1 9
```

d)
```
  6 6
+ 1 7
```

e)
```
  1 5
+ 3 8
```

f)
```
  1 3
+ 1 9
```

g)
```
  2 4
+ 3 8
```

h)
```
  5 4
+ 1 8
```

i)
```
  2 7
+ 6 9
```

j)
```
  4 6
+ 4 8
```

Step 2: Add the numbers in the tens column.

k)
```
  1
  1 2
+ 1 8
  3 0
```

l)
```
  1
  1 3
+ 1 7
    0
```

m)
```
  1
  1 5
+ 2 8
    3
```

n)
```
  1
  2 6
+ 2 6
    2
```

o)
```
  1
  3 8
+ 2 7
    5
```

3. Add the numbers with regrouping.

a)
```
  1
  3 6
+ 1 8
  5 4
```

b)
```
  3 7
+ 1 8
```

c)
```
  5 9
+ 1 8
```

d)
```
  3 7
+ 4 3
```

e)
```
  5 7
+ 2 6
```

f)
```
  6 3
+ 2 9
```

g)
```
  5 8
+ 4 7
```

h)
```
  1 8
+ 7 7
```

i)
```
  5 9
+ 1 3
```

j)
```
  7 5
+ 1 6
```

Sometimes the sum of two 2-digit numbers is a 3-digit number.

Example:

1		
	7	5
+	8	2
1	5	7

7 tens + 8 tens = 15 tens = 1 hundred + 5 tens, so we need to regroup 10 tens as 1 hundred.

4. Add, regrouping 10 tens as 1 hundred.

a)
1		
	7	5
+	8	2
1	5	7

b)
	8	4
+	6	3

c)
	7	2
+	6	5

d)
	9	1
+	9	6

e)
	8	5
+	7	3

5. Add, regrouping 10 ones as 1 ten and 10 tens as 1 hundred.

a)
1	1	
	7	5
+	6	7
1	4	2

b)
	8	6
+	3	9

c)
	5	8
+	4	7

d)
	7	6
+	7	8

e)
	3	5
+	6	5

You need to regroup 6 + 9 = 15 as 1 ten and 5 ones, but you can write 1 + 8 + 7 tens = 16 tens directly.

```
  1
  8 6
+ 7 9
-----
1 6 5
```

6. Add, regrouping when you need to.

a)
	8	5
+	3	4

b)
	7	4
+	2	8

c)
	7	9
+	8	8

d)
	6	4
+	3	9

e)
	7	5
+	2	5

7. Add with regrouping. Use grid paper.

a) 37 + 48   b) 29 + 83   c) 66 + 39   d) 75 + 48   e) 91 + 87

NS4-14 Addition Strategies

1. Add mentally.

   a) $10 + 5 =$ _____   b) $40 + 8 =$ _____   c) $9 + 50 =$ _____   d) $450 + 1 =$ _____

   e) $4 + 980 =$ _____   f) $900 + 19 =$ _____   g) $45 + 1200 =$ _____   h) $6 + 9800 =$ _____

2. Circle the pair that adds to 10. Write the number that is left over. Then finish adding.

   a) ④$+ 5 +$⑥$= 10 + \underline{\quad 5 \quad} =$ _____   b) $7 + 3 + 4 = 10 +$ _____ $=$ _____

   c) $8 + 3 + 2 = 10 +$ _____ $=$ _____   d) $6 + 9 + 4 = 10 +$ _____ $=$ _____

   e) $9 + 1 + 7 = 10 +$ _____ $=$ _____   f) $5 + 8 + 2 = 10 +$ _____ $=$ _____

Glen adds 5 to 7 by making 10.

$$7 + 5 = 7 + \underline{\quad 3 \quad} + \underline{\quad 2 \quad} = 10 + \underline{\quad 2 \quad} = \underline{\quad 12 \quad}$$

with the number bond showing 5 splitting into 3 and 2.

---

3. Add by making 10.

   8 (number bond above)

   a) $35 + 8 = 35 +$ _____ $+$ _____ $=$ _____ $+$ _____ $=$ _____

   b) $429 + 8 = 429 +$ _____ $+$ _____ $=$ _____ $+$ _____ $=$ _____

   c) $1256 + 7 = 1256 +$ _____ $+$ _____ $=$ _____ $+$ _____ $=$ _____

Sara adds 9 with tens blocks. She notices that she will have the same number of blocks if she adds 9 ones blocks or adds 1 tens block and then takes away a ones block.

$5 + 9 \quad = \quad 14$ $5 + 10 - 1 = 14$

---

4. Add 9 by adding 10, and then subtracting 1.

   a) $6 + 9 = \underline{\quad 16 \quad} - 1 = \underline{\quad 15 \quad}$ b) $8 + 9 =$ _____ $- 1 =$ _____

   c) $9 + 25 =$ _____ $- 1 =$ _____   d) $73 + 9 =$ _____ $- 1 =$ _____

   e) $9 + 257 =$ _____ $- 1 =$ _____   f) $1052 + 9 =$ _____ $- 1 =$ _____

5. Add 8 by adding 10, and then subtracting 2.

   a) $7 + 8 = \underline{\quad 17 \quad} - 2 =$ _____   b) $38 + 8 =$ _____ $- 2 =$ _____

   c) $8 + 146 =$ _____ $- 2 =$ _____   d) $8 + 245 =$ _____ $- 2 =$ _____

6. Add mentally.

   a) $64 + 9 =$ _____

   b) $489 + 9 =$ _____

   c) $64 + 8 =$ _____

   d) $275 + 8 =$ _____

   e) $3969 + 8 =$ _____

   f) $1397 + 9 =$ _____

7. Add 99 or 98 by adding 100, and then subtracting 1 or 2.

   a) $6 + 99 =$ _106_ $- 1 =$ _105_

   b) $8 + 98 =$ _____ $- 2 =$ _____

   c) $25 + 99 =$ _____ $- 1 =$ _____

   d) $37 + 98 =$ _____ $- 2 =$ _____

   e) $99 + 27 =$ _____ $- 1 =$ _____

   f) $98 + 63 =$ _____ $- 2 =$ _____

8. Add mentally.

   a) $73 + 99 =$ _____

   b) $98 + 257 =$ _____

   c) $1052 + 99 =$ _____

   d) $67 + 98 =$ _____

   e) $482 + 99 =$ _____

   f) $99 + 5871 =$ _____

9. Add by rounding up, adding, and then subtracting 1 or 2.

   a) $6 + 69 = 6 +$ _70_ $-$ _1_ $=$ _76_ $-$ _1_ $=$ _75_

   b) $43 + 58 = 43 +$ _____ $-$ _2_ $=$ _____ $-$ _2_ $=$ _____

   c) $25 + 78 = 25 +$ _____ $-$ _____ $=$ _____ $-$ _____ $=$ _____

   d) $29 + 49 = 29 +$ _____ $-$ _____ $=$ _____ $-$ _____ $=$ _____

10. There are 78 school days before the winter break and 116 days after. How many school days are there altogether?

11. Students in Ms. Jones' class sold tickets for the school play. On the first day, they sold 56 tickets. On the second day, they sold 99 tickets. On the third day, they sold 101 tickets. How many tickets did they sell altogether?

12. Zara sold 29 tickets to the school play on Wednesday and 34 tickets on Thursday. Evan sold 58 on Wednesday but only 7 on Thursday. Who sold more?

13. A large bus holds 98 students. How many students do 5 large buses hold?

14. Kim writes: $102 + 99 = 101 + 100 = 201$. Explain her method.

    BONUS ▶ Add by rounding up, adding, and then subtracting 3.

    a) $64 + 7$ b) $26 + 7$ c) $74 + 27$ d) $247 + 17$ BONUS ▶ $4515 + 67$

NS4-15 Adding Large Numbers

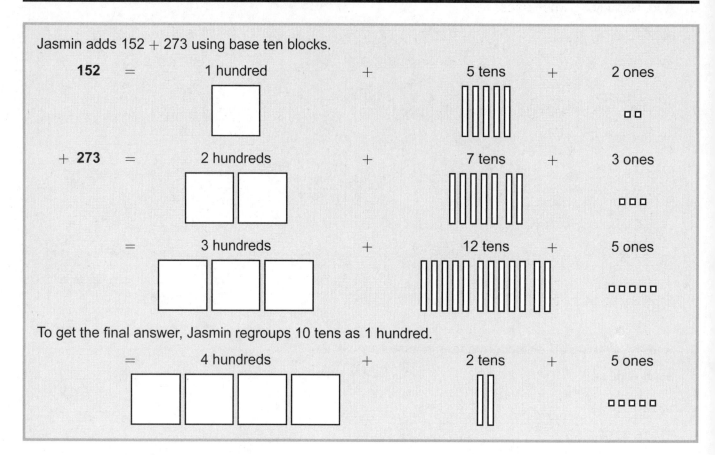

Jasmin adds 152 + 273 using base ten blocks.

| **152** | = | 1 hundred | + | 5 tens | + | 2 ones |

| + **273** | = | 2 hundreds | + | 7 tens | + | 3 ones |

| | = | 3 hundreds | + | 12 tens | + | 5 ones |

To get the final answer, Jasmin regroups 10 tens as 1 hundred.

| | = | 4 hundreds | + | 2 tens | + | 5 ones |

1. Add the numbers using expanded form.

a)   353   _____ hundreds + _____ tens + _____ ones

   + 164   + _____ hundred + _____ tens + _____ ones

             = _____ hundreds + _____ tens + _____ ones

   after regrouping   = _____ hundreds + _____ ten + _____ ones

b)   462   _____ hundreds + _____ tens + _____ ones

   + 375   + _____ hundreds + _____ tens + _____ ones

             = _____ hundreds + _____ tens + _____ ones

   after regrouping   = _____ hundreds + _____ tens + _____ ones

2. Add. You will need to regroup.

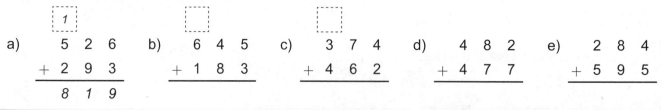

a)   ┌─1─┐
      5 2 6
    + 2 9 3
    ─────────
      8 1 9

b)   6 4 5
    + 1 8 3

c)   3 7 4
    + 4 6 2

d)   4 8 2
    + 4 7 7

e)   2 8 4
    + 5 9 5

3. Add, regrouping when necessary.

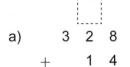

a)
```
    3  2  8
 +     1  4
 _____
```

b)
```
    7  4  7
 +  5  1  6
 _____
```

c)
```
    9  1  5
 +     4  5
 _____
```

d)
```
    3  4  6
 +  2  0  5
 _____
```

e)
```
    2  1  8
 +  3  4  8
 _____
```

f)
```
    5  6  4
 +  5  5  3
 _____
```

g)
```
    7  4  8
 +  4  2  4
 _____
```

h)
```
    7  2  6
 +  6  4  8
 _____
```

i)
```
    5  6  4
 +  6  7  2
 _____
```

j)
```
    4  4  4
 +  2  0  9
 _____
```

4. Line the numbers up correctly in the grid, then add.

a) 218 + 265   b) 272 + 213   c) 643 + 718   d) 937 + 25

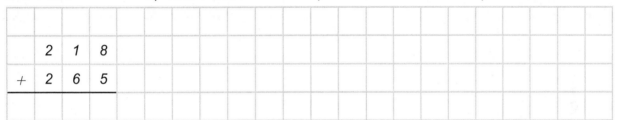

	2	1	8
+	2	6	5

e) 146 + 273   f) 816 + 925   g) 369 + 119   h) 847 + 910

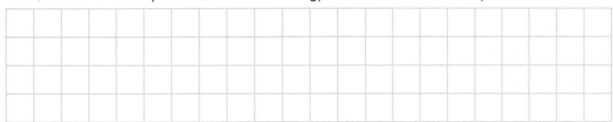

5. Add. You will need to regroup twice.

a)
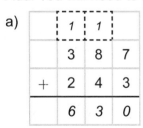

	1	1	
	3	8	7
+	2	4	3
	6	3	0

b)
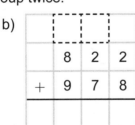

	8	2	2
+	9	7	8

c)
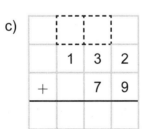

	1	3	2
+		7	9

d)
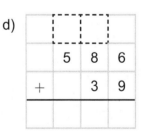

	5	8	6
+		3	9

BONUS ▶

Use the pattern in your answers to a), b), and c) to find the sums in d) and e) without adding.

a)
```
      9
 +    9
 _____
```

b)
```
    9  9
 +  9  9
 _____
```

c)
```
    9  9  9
 +  9  9  9
 _____
```

d)
```
    9  9  9  9
 +  9  9  9  9
 _____
```

e)
```
    9  9  9  9  9
 +  9  9  9  9  9
 _____
```

6. Add the numbers. Use grid paper.

a) 22 + 36 + 21   b) 324 + 112 + 422   c) 248 + 167 + 539

Avril adds 1852 + 2321 using base ten blocks.

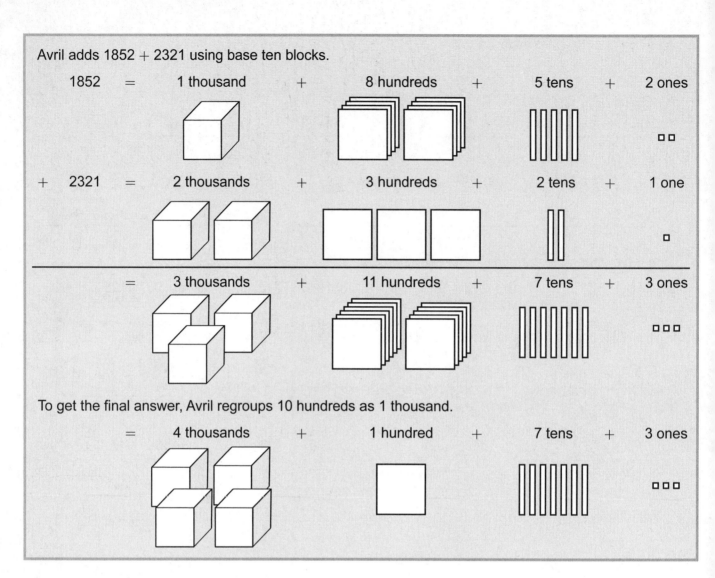

To get the final answer, Avril regroups 10 hundreds as 1 thousand.

7. Add the numbers using expanded form.

a) 2543   _____ thousands + _____ hundreds + _____ tens + _____ ones

   + 3621   + _____ thousands + _____ hundreds + _____ tens + _____ one

                  = _____ thousands + _____ hundreds + _____ tens + _____ ones

after regrouping   = _____ thousands + _____ hundred + _____ tens + _____ ones

b) 3824   _____ thousands + _____ hundreds + _____ tens + _____ ones

   + 1654   + _____ thousand + _____ hundreds + _____ tens + _____ ones

                  = _____ thousands + _____ hundreds + _____ tens + _____ ones

after regrouping   = _____ thousands + _____ hundreds + _____ tens + _____ ones

8. Add. You will need to regroup.

a)
```
  1
  5 2 6 5
+ 2 9 1 2
---------
  8 1 7 7
```

b)
```
  6 4 5 4
+ 1 8 3 3
---------
```

c)
```
  3 7 4 7
+ 2 6 2 1
---------
```

d)
```
  1 8 2 1
+ 2 7 7 2
---------
```

e)
```
  1 8 2 4
+ 5 7 7 3
---------
```

9. Add, regrouping when necessary.

a)
```
  2 3 5 4
+ 2 8 3 1
---------
```

b)
```
  9 6 8 3
+ 1 7 4 2
---------
```

c)
```
  5 8 7 1
+ 4 8 3 3
---------
```

d)
```
  8 5 2 5
+ 1 5 3 3
---------
```

e)
```
  9 8 7 9
+ 2 7 2 3
---------
```

f)
```
  7 5 4 6
+ 4 8 2 2
---------
```

g)
```
  7 6 2 4
+ 1 6 0 1
---------
```

h)
```
  6 6 9 0
+ 3 7 1 2
---------
```

i)
```
  9 9 7 5
+ 3 7 5 1
---------
```

j)
```
  3 9 4 5
+ 3 4 5 1
---------
```

k)
```
  4 5 3 4
+ 2 5 4 2
---------
```

l)
```
  6 7 5 4
+ 1 3 6 0
---------
```

m)
```
  3 2 1 4
+ 4 8 5 2
---------
```

n)
```
  2 5 0 9
+   6 2 1
---------
```

o)
```
  5 3 7 2
+   5 2 1
---------
```

p)
```
  6 8 2 7
+     8 5
---------
```

q)
```
  9 8 5 6
+   7 4 2
---------
```

r)
```
  4 3 2 1
+ 5 9 3 2
---------
```

s)
```
  6 2 3 1
+ 7 4 8 9
---------
```

t)
```
  8 0 3 2
+   5 1 8
---------
```

10. Add by lining up the digits correctly in the grid. You may have to regroup twice.

a) 2468 + 7431   b) 8596 + 1235   c) 6650 + 2198   d) 8359 + 48

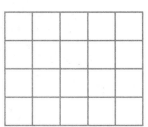 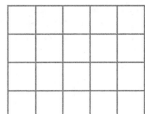 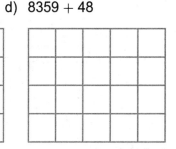

11. Add, regrouping when necessary.

a) 3326 + 1234 + 4762   b) 3658 + 1343 + 4534   c) 389 + 3247 + 712 + 52

NS4-16 Subtraction

To subtract 48 − 32, Braden makes a model of 48.

Then he crosses out 3 tens and 2 ones because 32 = 3 tens + 2 ones.

48   48 − 32   =   16

1. Subtract by crossing out tens and ones blocks. Draw your final answer in the right-hand box.

a)

39 − 18	= 21
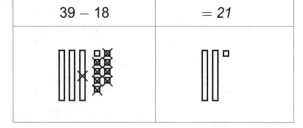	

b)

25 − 11	=

c)

43 − 21	=

d)

45 − 32	=

2. Write how many tens and ones in each number. Then subtract the tens and ones to find the final answer.

a) $45 = \underline{\ 4\ }$ tens $+ \underline{\ 5\ }$ ones

 $- 32 = \underline{\ 3\ }$ tens $+ \underline{\ 2\ }$ ones

 $= \underline{\ 1\ }$ ten $+ \underline{\ 3\ }$ ones

 $= \underline{\ \ 13\ \ }$

b) $57 = \underline{\ \ \ }$ tens $+ \underline{\ \ \ }$ ones

 $- 34 = \underline{\ \ \ }$ tens $+ \underline{\ \ \ }$ ones

 $= \underline{\ \ \ }$ tens $+ \underline{\ \ \ }$ ones

 $= \underline{\ \ \ \ \ \ }$

c) $84 = \underline{\ \ \ }$ tens $+ \underline{\ \ \ }$ ones

 $- 63 = \underline{\ \ \ }$ tens $+ \underline{\ \ \ }$ ones

 $= \underline{\ \ \ }$ tens $+ \underline{\ \ \ }$ one

 $= \underline{\ \ \ \ \ \ }$

d) $89 = \underline{\ \ \ }$ tens $+ \underline{\ \ \ }$ ones

 $- 56 = \underline{\ \ \ }$ tens $+ \underline{\ \ \ }$ ones

 $= \underline{\ \ \ }$ tens $+ \underline{\ \ \ }$ ones

 $= \underline{\ \ \ \ \ \ }$

e) $77 = \underline{\ \ \ }$ tens $+ \underline{\ \ \ }$ ones

 $- 44 = \underline{\ \ \ }$ tens $+ \underline{\ \ \ }$ ones

 $= \underline{\ \ \ }$ tens $+ \underline{\ \ \ }$ ones

 $= \underline{\ \ \ \ \ \ }$

f) $67 = \underline{\ \ \ }$ tens $+ \underline{\ \ \ }$ ones

 $- 45 = \underline{\ \ \ }$ tens $+ \underline{\ \ \ }$ ones

 $= \underline{\ \ \ }$ tens $+ \underline{\ \ \ }$ ones

 $= \underline{\ \ \ \ \ \ }$

3. Subtract by writing the number of tens and ones in each number.

a)
$$36 = 30 + 6$$
$$- \ 24 = 20 + 4$$
$$= 10 + 2$$
$$= 12$$

b)
$$84 =$$
$$- \ 52 =$$
$$=$$
$$=$$

c)
$$98 =$$
$$- \ 37 =$$
$$=$$
$$=$$

d)
$$73 =$$
$$- \ 12 =$$

e)
$$26 =$$
$$- \ 24 =$$

f)
$$88 =$$
$$- \ 33 =$$

4. Subtract the number by subtracting the digits.

a)
$$\begin{array}{r} 5 \ 4 \\ - \ 2 \ 3 \\ \hline \end{array}$$

b)
$$\begin{array}{r} 8 \ 6 \\ - \ 7 \ 3 \\ \hline \end{array}$$

c)
$$\begin{array}{r} 3 \ 6 \\ - \ 1 \ 5 \\ \hline \end{array}$$

d)
$$\begin{array}{r} 6 \ 4 \\ - \ 3 \ 2 \\ \hline \end{array}$$

e)
$$\begin{array}{r} 9 \ 5 \\ - \ 4 \ 2 \\ \hline \end{array}$$

f)
$$\begin{array}{r} 8 \ 9 \\ - \ 4 \ 0 \\ \hline \end{array}$$

5. a) Draw a picture of 543 using hundreds, tens, and ones blocks.
Show how you would subtract 543 − 421.

b) Now subtract 543 − 421 by lining up the digits and subtracting. Do you get the same answer?

6. Subtract.

a)
$$\begin{array}{r} 7 \ 5 \ 3 \ 2 \\ - \ 4 \ 1 \ 2 \ 1 \\ \hline \end{array}$$

b)
$$\begin{array}{r} 5 \ 3 \ 5 \ 6 \\ - \ 4 \ 2 \ 4 \ 5 \\ \hline \end{array}$$

c)
$$\begin{array}{r} 5 \ 7 \ 6 \ 3 \\ - \ 3 \ 0 \ 1 \ 1 \\ \hline \end{array}$$

Jax subtracts 46 − 18 using base ten blocks.

Step 1:
Jax represents 46 with base ten blocks.

Step 2:
8 (the ones digit of 18) is greater than 6 (the ones digit of 46) so Jax regroups 1 tens block as 10 ones blocks.

Step 3:
Jax subtracts 18 (he takes away 1 tens block and 8 ones blocks).

Tens	Ones
4	6

Here is how Jax uses numerals to show his work:

$$\begin{array}{r} 46 \\ -\,18 \\ \hline \end{array}$$

Tens	Ones
3	16

Here is how Jax shows the regrouping:

$$\begin{array}{r} {}^{3}\,{}^{16} \\ \cancel{4}\,\cancel{6} \\ -\,1\,8 \\ \hline \end{array}$$

Tens	Ones
2	8

And now Jax can subtract 16 − 8 ones and 3 − 1 tens:

$$\begin{array}{r} {}^{3}\,{}^{16} \\ \cancel{4}\,\cancel{6} \\ -\,1\,8 \\ \hline 2\,8 \end{array}$$

1. Regroup 1 tens block as 10 ones. Then change the subtraction statement.

a) **63 − 26**

Tens	Ones		Tens	Ones
6	3		5	13

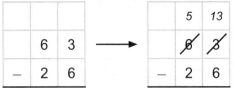

b) **64 − 39**

Tens	Ones		Tens	Ones
6	4			

$$\begin{array}{cc} 6 & 4 \\ -\,3 & 9 \end{array} \longrightarrow \begin{array}{cc} 6 & 4 \\ -\,3 & 9 \end{array}$$

c) **42 − 19**

Tens	Ones		Tens	Ones
4	2			

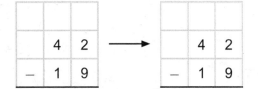

d) **35 − 27**

Tens	Ones		Tens	Ones
3	5			

$$\begin{array}{cc} 3 & 5 \\ -\,2 & 7 \end{array} \longrightarrow \begin{array}{cc} 3 & 5 \\ -\,2 & 7 \end{array}$$

2. Subtract with regrouping.

a)
	3	13
	~~4~~	~~3~~
−	2	7
	1	6

b)
	5	6
−	1	8

c)
	6	4
−	3	9

d)
	7	0
−	2	8

e)
	5	5
−	3	7

f)
	8	0
−	5	7

g)
	3	8
−	1	9

h)
	2	2
−		6

i)
	4	4
−		9

j)
	9	0
−	7	5

3. If you need to regroup, write "regroup" in the blank. If you don't need to regroup, write "OK." Then find the answer.

a)
$$\begin{array}{r} {\scriptstyle 4\ 14} \\ \cancel{5}\cancel{4} \\ -\ 1\ 9 \\ \hline 3\ 5 \end{array}$$
____regroup____
4 is less than 9

b)
$$\begin{array}{r} 7\ 7 \\ -\ 5\ 6 \\ \hline \end{array}$$
____OK____

c)
$$\begin{array}{r} 8\ 5 \\ -\ 5\ 3 \\ \hline \end{array}$$
_____

d)
$$\begin{array}{r} 9\ 5 \\ -\ 1\ 8 \\ \hline \end{array}$$
_____

e)
$$\begin{array}{r} 6\ 6 \\ -\ 5\ 4 \\ \hline \end{array}$$
_____

f)
$$\begin{array}{r} 8\ 4 \\ -\ 1\ 7 \\ \hline \end{array}$$
_____

g)
$$\begin{array}{r} 8\ 2 \\ -\ 2\ 9 \\ \hline \end{array}$$
_____

h)
$$\begin{array}{r} 2\ 6 \\ -\ 1\ 5 \\ \hline \end{array}$$
_____

i)
$$\begin{array}{r} 4\ 5 \\ -\ \ \ 9 \\ \hline \end{array}$$
_____

j)
$$\begin{array}{r} 1\ 2 \\ -\ \ \ 8 \\ \hline \end{array}$$
_____

k)
$$\begin{array}{r} 3\ 0 \\ -\ 1\ 9 \\ \hline \end{array}$$
_____

l)
$$\begin{array}{r} 5\ 2 \\ -\ \ \ 9 \\ \hline \end{array}$$
_____

m)
$$\begin{array}{r} 4\ 7 \\ -\ 1\ 9 \\ \hline \end{array}$$
_____

n)
$$\begin{array}{r} 2\ 3 \\ -\ \ \ 8 \\ \hline \end{array}$$
_____

o)
$$\begin{array}{r} 6\ 0 \\ -\ 4\ 9 \\ \hline \end{array}$$
_____

p)
$$\begin{array}{r} 8\ 0 \\ -\ 4\ 1 \\ \hline \end{array}$$
_____

q)
$$\begin{array}{r} 9\ 3 \\ -\ 2\ 4 \\ \hline \end{array}$$
_____

r)
$$\begin{array}{r} 7\ 9 \\ -\ 4\ 2 \\ \hline \end{array}$$
_____

4. Subtract, regrouping 1 hundred as 10 tens.

a)

	2	11	
	3̷	1̷	5
−	1	6	2

b)

	5	3	8
−	2	9	5

c)

	3	1	7
−	1	8	6

d)

	9	4	2
−	5	7	0

Yu subtracts 854 − 367 by following these steps:

Step 1

```
    4 14
  8 5̷ 4̷
− 3 6 7
```

Step 2

```
    4 14
  8 5̷ 4̷
− 3 6 7
        7
```

Step 3

```
      14
  7 4̷ 14
  8̷ 5̷ 4̷
− 3 6 7
        7
```

Step 4

```
      14
  7 4̷ 14
  8̷ 5̷ 4̷
− 3 6 7
      8 7
```

Step 5

```
      14
  7 4̷ 14
  8̷ 5̷ 4̷
− 3 6 7
    4 8 7
```

5. Subtract, regrouping twice.

a)

	6	3	4
−	1	5	6

b)

	5	8	5
−		9	6

c)

	5	3	2
−	2	3	5

d)

	8	5	4
−	3	7	7

e)

	5	2	7
−	3	8	8

f)

	9	1	5
−	6	4	6

g)

	1	3	2
−		4	7

h)

	6	3	4	2
−	2	1	5	8

i)

	8	6	5
−	3	9	7

j)

	7	2	0
−	4	4	5

k)

	6	0	3
−	2	4	8

l)

	5	4	1	0
−	1	1	2	3

6. Subtract, regrouping 1 thousand as 10 hundreds.

a)

	7	13		
	8̷	3̷	6	4
−	4	8	3	1
	3	5	3	3

b)

	5	6	9	3
−	2	7	1	1

c)

	5	7	5	8
−	2	9	4	2

NS4-18 Subtraction Strategies

1. Subtract mentally.

   a) 9 − 5 = _____   b) 29 − 6 = _____   c) 38 − 4 = _____   d) 57 − 2 = _____

   e) 459 − 6 = _____   f) 787 − 3 = _____   g) 986 − 4 = _____   h) 679 − 7 = _____

   i) 1928 − 5 = _____   j) 1259 − 4 = _____   k) 9867 − 5 = _____   l) 1028 − 3 = _____

2. Subtract the ones, then subtract the rest.

   a) 46 − 9 = 46 − __6__ − __3__ = __40__ − __3__ = _____

   b) 53 − 6 = 53 − __3__ − _____ = _____ − _____ = _____

   c) 72 − 8 = 72 − _____ − _____ = _____ − _____ = _____

   d) 65 − 7 = 65 − _____ − _____ = _____ − _____ = _____

   e) 103 − 6 = 103 − _____ − _____ = _____ − _____ = _____

   f) 245 − 9 = 245 − _____ − _____ = _____ − _____ = _____

3. Subtract mentally.

   a) 23 − 4 = _____   b) 31 − 3 = _____   c) 42 − 4 = _____   d) 65 − 6 = _____

   e) 58 − 9 = _____   f) 76 − 8 = _____   g) 95 − 7 = _____   h) 84 − 5 = _____

4. Subtract 9 by subtracting 10, and then adding 1.

   a) 42 − 9 = (42 − __10__) + 1 = __32__ + 1 = __33__

   b) 57 − 9 = (57 − __10__) + 1 = _____ + 1 = _____

   c) 64 − 9 = (64 − _____) + 1 = _____ + 1 = _____

   d) 73 − 9 = (73 − _____) + 1 = _____ + 1 = _____

   e) 81 − 9 = (81 − _____) + 1 = _____ + 1 = _____

   f) 95 − 9 = (95 − _____) + 1 = _____ + 1 = _____

   g) 33 − 9 = _____ + 1 = _____   h) 26 − 9 = _____ + 1 = _____

5. Subtract mentally.

   a) 48 − 9 = _____   b) 76 − 9 = _____   c) 37 − 9 = _____   d) 52 − 9 = _____

   e) 61 − 9 = _____   f) 80 − 9 = _____   g) 53 − 9 = _____   h) 24 − 9 = _____

6. Subtract 8 by subtracting 10, and then adding 2.

   a) $42 - 8 = (42 - \underline{\;10\;}) + 2 = \underline{\;32\;} + 2 = \underline{\;34\;}$

   b) $57 - 8 = (57 - \underline{\;10\;}) + 2 = \underline{} + 2 = \underline{}$

   c) $65 - 8 = (65 - \underline{}) + 2 = \underline{} + 2 = \underline{}$

   d) $96 - 8 = (96 - \underline{}) + 2 = \underline{} + 2 = \underline{}$

   e) $23 - 8 = \underline{} + 2 = \underline{}$ f) $84 - 8 = \underline{} + 2 = \underline{}$

7. Subtract mentally.

   a) $46 - 8 = \underline{}$ b) $75 - 8 = \underline{}$ c) $57 - 8 = \underline{}$ d) $22 - 8 = \underline{}$

   e) $31 - 8 = \underline{}$ f) $60 - 8 = \underline{}$ g) $93 - 8 = \underline{}$ h) $14 - 8 = \underline{}$

8. Subtract 19 by subtracting 20, and then adding 1.

   a) $42 - 19 = (42 - \underline{\;20\;}) + 1 = \underline{\;22\;} + 1 = \underline{\;23\;}$

   b) $57 - 19 = (57 - \underline{\;20\;}) + 1 = \underline{} + 1 = \underline{}$

   c) $64 - 19 = (64 - \underline{}) + 1 = \underline{} + 1 = \underline{}$

   d) $73 - 19 = (73 - \underline{}) + 1 = \underline{} + 1 = \underline{}$

   e) $95 - 19 = (95 - \underline{}) + \underline{} = \underline{} + \underline{} = \underline{}$

   f) $281 - 19 = \underline{} + \underline{\;1\;} = \underline{}$ g) $326 - 19 = \underline{} + \underline{} = \underline{}$

9. Subtract by rounding up, and then adding 1 or 2.

   a) $62 - 49 = (62 - \underline{\;50\;}) + \underline{\;1\;} = \underline{\;12\;} + \underline{\;1\;} = \underline{\;13\;}$

   b) $57 - 28 = (57 - \underline{\;30\;}) + \underline{\;2\;} = \underline{} + \underline{\;2\;} = \underline{}$

   c) $64 - 38 = (64 - \underline{}) + \underline{} = \underline{} + \underline{} = \underline{}$

   d) $73 - 59 = (73 - \underline{}) + \underline{} = \underline{} + \underline{} = \underline{}$

   e) $281 - 29 = (281 - \underline{}) + \underline{} = \underline{} + \underline{} = \underline{}$

   f) $95 - 78 = (95 - \underline{}) + \underline{} = \underline{} + \underline{} = \underline{}$

10. Ronin has 34 stickers. He bought 48 more stickers for his sticker collection. He gave 39 stickers to his brother. How many stickers does he have now?

11. Josh is reading a book that is 214 pages long. He reads 9 pages each night. How many pages will he have left after 3 nights?

12. 264 students are going to travel by bus on a school trip. Each bus holds 98 students. If the first two buses are full, how many students are on the third bus?

Subtracting from 100 and 1000

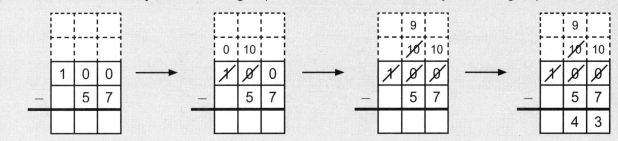

To subtract from 100, you need to regroup from the hundreds before you can regroup from the tens.

1. a) Subtract by regrouping.

i) 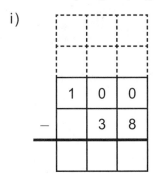 ii) 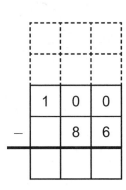 iii) 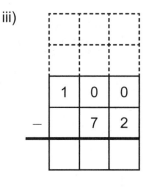 iv)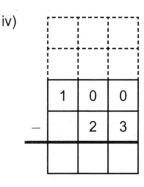

b) Subtract from 99 without regrouping.

i)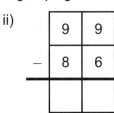

	9	9
−	3	8
	6	1

ii)
	9	9
−	8	6

iii)
	9	9
−	7	2

iv)
	9	9
−	2	3

c) How do your answers to part a) and part b) compare? Why is this the case?

To subtract from 100 or 1000, first subtract from 99 or 999. Then add 1.

$$99 \xrightarrow{\text{add } 1} 100$$
$$\frac{-\ 27}{72} \xrightarrow{\text{add } 1} \frac{-\ 27}{73}$$

$$999 \xrightarrow{\text{add } 1} 1000$$
$$\frac{-\ 346}{653} \xrightarrow{\text{add } 1} \frac{-\ 346}{654}$$

2. Subtract by using 99 or 999.

a) 100 − 28

	9	9
−	2	8

so 100 − 28 = _____

b) 1000 − 247

	9	9	9
−	2	4	7

so 1000 − 247 = _____

c) 1000 − 762

d) 1000 − 84

BONUS ▶

10 000 − 8290

NS4-20 Estimating Sums and Differences

Mathematicians use the sign ≈ to mean **approximately equal to**.

1. Estimate by rounding to the nearest **ten**.

a) 52 → $\boxed{50}$ b) 19 $\boxed{}$ c) 47 $\boxed{}$ d) 95 $\boxed{}$

   $\underline{+\,34}$ → + $\boxed{30}$ $\underline{+\,65}$ + $\boxed{}$ $\underline{+\,11}$ + $\boxed{}$ $\underline{-\,62}$ − $\boxed{}$

   $\boxed{80}$ $\boxed{}$ $\boxed{}$ $\boxed{}$

e) 32 + 11   f) 74 + 32   g) 37 + 25   h) 84 + 28

   ≈ _30 + 10_   ≈ _____   ≈ _____   ≈ _____

   = _40_   = _____   = _____   = _____

i) 25 + 37 + 59   j) 28 − 12   k) 36 + 63 + 72   l) 85 − 17

   ≈ _____   ≈ _____   ≈ _____   ≈ _____

   = _____   = _____   = _____   = _____

2. Estimate by rounding to the nearest **hundred**.

a) 170 $\boxed{200}$ b) 190 $\boxed{}$ c) 470 $\boxed{}$ d) 950 $\boxed{}$

   $\underline{+\,350}$ + $\boxed{400}$ $\underline{+\,650}$ + $\boxed{}$ $\underline{-\,110}$ − $\boxed{}$ $\underline{-\,620}$ − $\boxed{}$

   $\boxed{600}$ $\boxed{}$ $\boxed{}$ $\boxed{}$

e) 540 + 210   f) 550 + 330   g) 210 + 770   h) 750 + 220

   ≈ _____   ≈ _____   ≈ _____   ≈ _____

   = _____   = _____   = _____   = _____

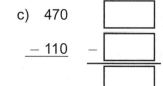 i) 380 + 420 + 190   j) 871 − 543   k) 483 + 283   l) 689 − 214

3. Estimate by rounding to the nearest **thousand**.

a) 1275 $\boxed{1000}$ b) 4729 $\boxed{}$ c) 2570 $\boxed{}$ d) 9172 $\boxed{}$

   $\underline{+\,3940}$ + $\boxed{4000}$ $\underline{+\,3132}$ + $\boxed{}$ $\underline{+\,634}$ + $\boxed{}$ $\underline{-\,4529}$ − $\boxed{}$

   $\boxed{5000}$ $\boxed{}$ $\boxed{}$ $\boxed{}$

4. Round each number to the nearest **hundred**. Then find the sum or difference.

a) 3272 + 1235   b) 3581 − 1826   c) 4821 − 3670

5. Lewis collected 75 books for charity and Emma collected 18 books. About how many did they collect altogether?

6. Class 4A collected 287 books and class 4B collected 476 books for charity.

a) About how many books did 4A and 4B collect altogether?

b) Is your estimate higher or lower than the actual answer? How do you know?

7. A store has the following items for sale:

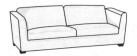

Sofa $472   Armchair $227   Table $189   Desk $382   Lamp $112

What could you buy if you had $800 to spend? Estimate to find out.
Then add the actual prices to check your estimate.

8. Ansel estimates $432 + 512$ as $400 + 500 = 900$.

a) Calculate the actual sum.

b) Is Ansel's estimate higher or lower than the actual sum?
Why does this make sense?

9. Tess adds numbers. Use estimation to decide whether her answers are reasonable.

a) $378 + 463 = 1021$ b) $3516 + 4209 = 7725$ c) $2435 + 3351 = 4786$

10. Round the number to each place value.

		Tens	Hundreds	Thousands
a)	3485			
b)	8502			
	BONUS ▶ 9697			

BONUS ▶ Write every number that fits all three statements.

When rounded to the nearest ten, it is 6500.
When rounded to the nearest hundred, it is 6500.
When rounded to the nearest thousand, it is 6000.

BONUS ▶ The estimated difference between two numbers is 400.
What might the original numbers be?

A **centimetre** (**cm**) is a unit of measurement for **length** (or **height** or **thickness**).

•———• 1 cm

1. Measure the distance between the arrows.

a) 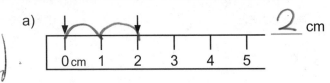 _2_ cm

b) 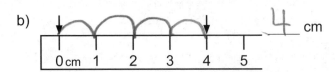 _4_ cm

c) 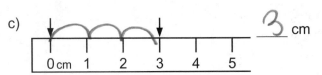 _3_ cm

d) 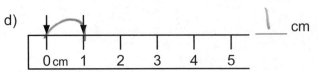 _1_ cm

BONUS ▶

e) 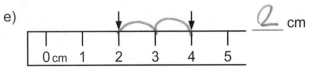 _2_ cm

f) 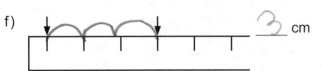 _3_ cm

2. Measure the length of the line segment or object.

a) 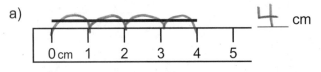 _4_ cm

b) 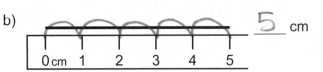 _5_ cm

c) 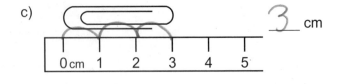 _3_ cm

d) 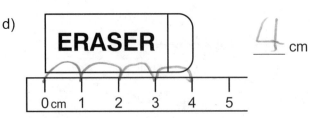 _4_ cm

BONUS ▶

e)  _3_ cm

f) 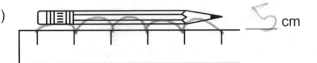 _5_ cm

3. Measure the length of the strip. Use a ruler.

a) _9_ cm

b) _13_ cm

c) _12_ cm

d) _8_ cm

4. Measure the length of the object. Use a ruler.

a) 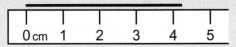 _3_ cm

b) _2_ cm

You can measure length **to the closest** centimetre. These line segments are **about** 4 cm long.

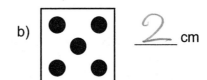

5. Measure the length of the strip to the closest centimetre. Use a ruler.

a) _11_ cm

b) _8 half_ cm

c) _9 half_ cm

6. Measure all the sides of the shape.

a)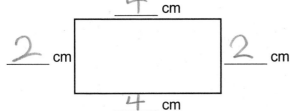

_4_ cm

_2_ cm   _2_ cm

_4_ cm

b)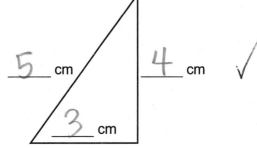

_5_ cm   _4_ cm ✓

_3_ cm

7. Draw two arrows to show the given distance.

a) 4 cm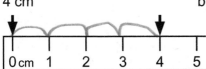

b) 3 cm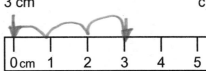

c) 5 cm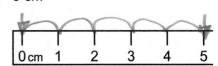

8. Draw a line segment of the given length.

a) 1 cm

| 0 cm | 1 | 2 | 3 | 4 | 5 |

b) 4 cm

| 0 cm | 1 | 2 | 3 | 4 | 5 |

c) 2 cm

| 0 cm | 1 | 2 | 3 | 4 | 5 |

d) 3 cm

e) 5 cm

f) 10 cm

9. Draw the object to the exact measurement.

a) a caterpillar, 4 cm long   b) a leaf, 6 cm wide   c) a tree, 8 cm tall

10. On grid paper, draw a rectangle with a length of 5 cm and a width of 2 cm. Use a ruler.

ME4-2 Millimetres

A **millimetre** (**mm**) is another unit of measurement for length (or height or thickness).

1 centimetre = 10 millimetres
1 cm = 10 mm

1. Fill in the measurements in millimetres.

cm	1	2	3	4	5	6	7	8
mm	10							

2. Which two multiples of 10 is the number between?

   a) 53: __50__ and __60__   b) 75: _____ and _____   c) 102: _____ and _____

   d) 254: _____ and _____   e) 2348: _____ and _____   f) 8706: _____ and _____

3. Underline the digits that show the number of whole centimetres in the measurement.

   a) <u>80</u>9 mm   b) 60 mm   c) 84 mm   d) 530 mm   e) 703 mm   f) 1682 mm

4. Underline the digits that show the number of whole centimetres in the measurement in millimetres. Then circle the larger measurement.

   a) 5 cm   (<u>70</u> mm)   b) 83 cm   <u>910</u> mm   c) 45 cm   53 mm

   d) 2 cm   12 mm   e) 60 cm   6200 mm   f) 72 cm   420 mm

   g) 1000 mm   105 cm   h) 3567 mm   350 cm   i) 9999 mm   999 cm

   BONUS ▶ Which is longer, 35 cm or 357 mm? How do you know? _____

   _____

A loonie is about 2 mm high. So a stack of five loonies would be about 1 cm high.

▭ 1 loonie = 2 mm   5 loonies = 10 mm = 1 cm

5. How many centimetres tall is the stack of loonies? Show your work.

   a) 10 loonies: _____ cm   b) 20 loonies: _____ cm   c) 40 loonies: _____ cm

Jessica wants to mark off 23 mm.

It is hard to count every millimetre. Jessica counts by 10s until she reaches 20 mm or 2 cm. Then she counts millimetres by 1s.

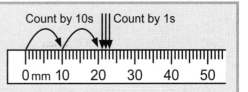

6. What is the distance between the two arrows?

a)

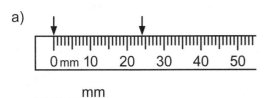

_____ mm

b)

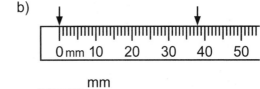

_____ mm

7. Find the length of the strip.

a)

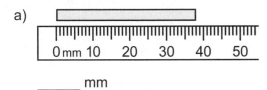

_____ mm

b)

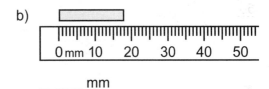

_____ mm

c)

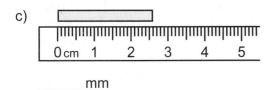

_____ mm

d)

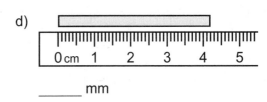

_____ mm

8. Draw a second arrow to show where a line segment of the given length would end.

a) 32 mm

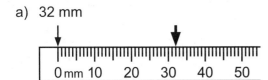

b) 18 mm

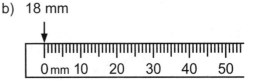

c) 26 mm

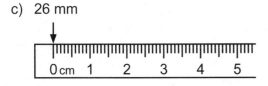

d) 19 mm

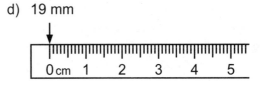

9. Draw a line segment of the given length.

a) 16 mm

b) 41 mm

10. Use a ruler to draw the object to the exact millimetre.

a) a pencil 50 mm long

b) a house 25 mm tall

c) a flower 27 mm wide

d) a beetle 32 mm long

ME4-3 Estimating

1. Your finger is about 1 cm (or 10 mm) wide. Measure the picture with your finger, then estimate the length in centimetres and in millimetres.

a)

ERASER

The eraser is about _____ cm long.

So the eraser is about _____ mm long.

b)

The crayon is about _____ cm long.

So the crayon is about _____ mm long.

c)

The pencil is about _____ cm long.

So the pencil is about _____ mm long.

d)

The tack is about _____ cm long.

So the tack is about _____ mm long.

2. Estimate if the strip is **less than** or **more than** 30 mm long. Put a check mark in the correct column.

	Less Than 30 mm	More Than 30 mm
a)		
b)		
c)		
d)		

3. How good were your estimates? Measure the length of each strip in Question 2.

a) _____ mm   b) _____ mm   c) _____ mm   d) _____ mm

4. Is the distance between the lines less than 20 mm? Write **yes** or **no**. Estimate, then measure the **actual** distance in millimetres.

	Less Than 20 mm	Estimate (mm)	Actual Distance (mm)
a)			
b)			
c)			
d)			

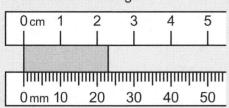

This rectangle is 23 mm long.
It is about 2 cm long.

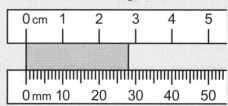

This rectangle is 28 mm long.
It is about 3 cm long.

5. Measure the line segment in centimetres and millimetres.

a) ─────────────

about _____ cm

or _____ mm

b) ──────

about _____ cm

or _____ mm

c)

about _____ cm

or _____ mm

d)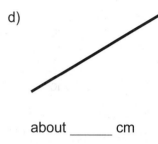

about _____ cm

or _____ mm

6. Measure the sides of the rectangle in centimetres. Then measure the distance along the dashed line between the opposite corners in centimetres and millimetres.

a)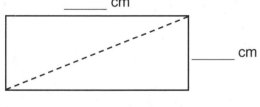

_____ cm

_____ cm

Dashed line = about _____ cm

= _____ mm

b)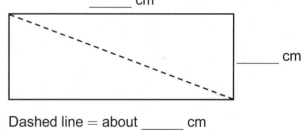

_____ cm

_____ cm

Dashed line = about _____ cm

= _____ mm

7. a) Estimate the width and the length of the rectangle in centimetres and in millimetres.

A

B

A: Length _____ cm, _____ mm

Width _____ cm, _____ mm

B: Length _____ cm, _____ mm

Width _____ cm, _____ mm

b) Measure the width and length of the rectangle in millimetres with a ruler.

A: Length _____ cm, _____ mm

Width _____ cm, _____ mm

B: Length _____ cm, _____ mm

Width _____ cm, _____ mm

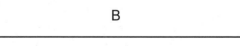 c) How close were your estimates in part a)?

ME4-4 Metres

A **metre** (**m**) is a unit of measurement for length (or height or thickness). 1 m = 100 cm.

A metre stick is about 100 cm long.

1. a) Measure the length of your classroom in giant steps. Try to make the giant steps the same length.

   Length = _____ giant steps

   b) Measure the length of your classroom in metres. Length = _____ metres

   c) Is your giant step longer than a metre or shorter than a metre? _____

   d) Can you use giant steps to estimate distance in metres? _____

2. a) Stretch your arms out. The distance between the tips of your fingers is called your **arm span**.

   Ask a friend to measure your arm span with a piece of string.

   Arm span = _____ cm

   Is your arm span more or less than a metre? _____

   b) Stretch your arms out. Fold them as shown. The distance between your elbows is called your **elbow span**.

   Ask a friend to measure your elbow span with a measuring tape.

   Elbow span = _____ cm

   Is your elbow span more or less than a metre? _____

   c) Stretch your arms out. Fold one arm as shown. The distance from one elbow to the tips of the fingers on the other hand is called your **arm-and-elbow span**.

   Ask a friend to measure your arm-and-elbow span with a piece of string.

   Arm-and-elbow span = _____ cm

   Is your arm-and-elbow span more or less than a metre? _____

   d) Which distance is closest to 1 metre? _____

3. a) Measure your height in centimetres. Height = _____ cm

   Are you taller than 1 metre? _____

   b) Measure the distance from your armpit to the floor. _____ cm

   Is this distance more than 1 metre? _____

   c) Which distance is better for estimating height in metres? _____

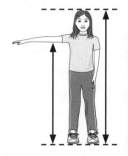

4. Estimate the length or the distance in metres. Measure the length or the distance using a metre stick or a measuring tape.

		Estimate	Actual Measurement
a)	Length of a board		
b)	Height of a door		
c)	Width of a window		
d)	Distance from a window to a door		
e)	Width of a carpet		
f)	Distance from a door to a cupboard		
g)	You choose:		

5. Fill in the measurements in centimetres.

m	1	2	3	4	5	6	7	8
cm	100							

6. How many whole hundreds?

a) 531: __5__ hundreds   b) 400: _____ hundreds   c) 108: _____ hundred

d) 2500: _____ hundreds   e) 2008: _____ hundreds   f) 84: _____ hundreds

7. Underline the digit or digits that show the number of whole metres.

a) <u>8</u>09 cm   b) 619 cm   c) 789 cm   d) 1540 cm   e) 3703 cm   f) 182 cm

8. Underline the digits that show the number of whole metres in the measurement in centimetres. Then circle the greater measurement.

a) <u>5</u>00 cm   (7 m)   b) 830 cm   91 m   c) 245 cm   5 m

d) 2222 cm   12 m   e) 60 m   6200 cm   f) 72 m   4203 cm

g) 9999 cm   9 m   h) 999 m   9999 cm   i) 99 m   9999 cm

9. What is longer, 8 m or 845 cm? How do you know? _____

_____

_____

Measurement 4-4   **57**

Ethan uses a metre stick to measure the length of the board. The board is more than 2 m long.

Ethan measures the leftover length in centimetres. The board is 2 m 70 cm long.

A measurement in two units is called a **mixed measurement**.

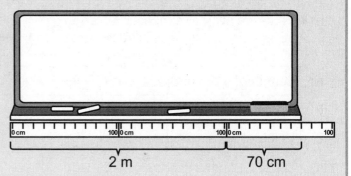

2 m   70 cm

10. Measure in metres and centimetres.

a) Length of a board   _____ m _____ cm

b) Height of a door   _____ m _____ cm

c) Width of a window   _____ m _____ cm

d) Distance from a window to a door   _____ m _____ cm

e) Width of a carpet   _____ m _____ cm

f) Distance from a door to a cupboard   _____ m _____ cm

11. Sun measured the height of her bedroom window with both a metre stick and a measuring tape.

• When she measured with the metre stick, the window was 2 m with 15 cm extra.
• When she measured with the measuring tape, the measurement was 215 cm.

Is there a difference in the two measurements? Explain.

_____

_____

12. Write the measurement as a mixed measurement in metres and centimetres.

a) 513 cm = __5__ m __13__ cm   b) 217 cm = _____ m _____ cm

c) 367 cm = _____ m _____ cm   d) 481 cm = _____ m _____ cm

e) 706 cm = _____ m _____ cm   f) 303 cm = _____ m _____ cm

13. Write a measurement in centimetres that is between the two measurements.

a) 4 m and 5 m   b) 9 m and 10 m   c) 25 m and 26 m

14. Write a measurement in metres that is between the two measurements.

a) 234 cm and 357 cm   b) 89 cm and 140 cm   c) 4025 cm and 5921 cm

We measure large distances in **kilometres** (**km**). 1 km = 1000 m.

1. a) 1000 = _____ hundreds = _____ tens = _____ ones

    b) A football field is about 100 m long. How many football fields long is a kilometre? _____

    c) A school bus is about 10 m long. How many school buses can park end to end

        along a 1 km distance? _____

2. a) You can walk 1 km in about 15 minutes. Name a place that is about 1 km from
        your school or home.

        _____

    b) It takes Avril 30 minutes to walk from home to school. About how many kilometres

        from school does Avril live? _____

    c) It takes Raj 42 minutes to walk from home to school. About how many kilometres

        from school does Raj live? _____

3. a) What is longer, 1001 m or 1 km? How do you know? _____

        _____

    b) Ella thinks that 6 km is shorter than 350 m because 6 is less than 350. Is she correct?

        Explain. _____

        _____

4. Fill in the table.

km	1	2	3	4	5	6	7	8
m	1000							

5. a) Write a measurement in metres that is between 5 km and 6 km. _____

    b) Write a measurement in kilometres that is between 3790 m and 4258 m. _____

6. How many whole kilometres are in the measurement?

    a) 3456 m   _3 km_   b) 8721 m _____   c) 6004 m _____   d) 987 m _____

7. Underline the number of whole kilometres in the measurement in metres. Circle the
    shorter measurement.

    a) (2106 m)   3 km   b) 8372 m   9 km   c) 6 km   6008 m   d) 9 km   945 m

8. a) Is the object less than 1 m long, about 1 m long, or more than 1 m long?

   i) coin _____   ii) baseball bat _____

   iii) canoe paddle _____   iv) small car _____

   b) Suppose the objects are lined up end to end. Is the line less than 10 km long,
       about 10 km long, or more than 10 km long?

   i) 10 000 coins _____   ii) 10 000 baseball bats _____

   iii) 10 000 canoe paddles _____   iv) 10 000 small cars _____

   BONUS ▶ A canoe is 3 m long. How long is a line of 10 000 canoes lined up end to end? _____

9. A track is 400 m long. Fill in the T-table.

   a) Jin ran around the track twice.

       How many metres did he run? _____

       Did he run at least 1 km? _____

   b) Jin wants to run 1500 m. About how many

       laps must he run around the track? _____

   c) How many laps must Jin run around

       the track to cover 2 km? _____

Laps Around the Track	Distance Covered (m)
1	400
2	

10. Use the map to write the distance between the places.

    a) St. John's and Gander _____ km

    b) Deer Lake and Port aux Basques _____ km

    c) Deer Lake and L'Anse aux Meadows _____ km

11. Use the map to answer the question.

    a) Gander is 27 km closer to Deer Lake than to St. John's.
        How far from Gander is Deer Lake?

    b) Tristan drives from St. John's to L'Anse aux Meadows
        Historic Site through Gander and Deer Lake.
        How far does he drive?

    c) Which distance is longer, from Port aux Basques
        to L'Anse aux Meadows through Deer Lake,
        or from St. John's to Deer Lake?

L'Anse aux Meadows
435 km
Atlantic Ocean
Deer Lake
Gander
266 km
333 km
Port aux Basques
St. John's

ME4-6 Selecting the Best Unit

1. a) Use the line below to mark two dots that are 115 mm apart. Do not use a ruler.

   b) Use a ruler to draw a line segment 115 mm long under the line above. Was your estimate too long, too short, or pretty close? _____

> **Decimetre (dm)** is a unit of measurement between metres and centimetres.
>
> 1 dm = 10 cm
>
> 1 m = 10 dm
>
> Your hand with fingers slightly apart is about 1 dm wide.
>
>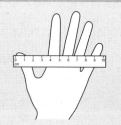

2. Fill in the table.

m	1	2	3	4	5	6
dm	10	20				
cm	100					
mm	1000					

3. a) 1 cm = _____ mm　　　b) 1 m = _____ cm　　　c) 1 m = _____ mm

> A dime is about 1 mm thick.
>
> Your finger is about 1 cm wide.
>
> A giant step is about 1 m long.
>
> 10 football fields are about 1 km long.
>
> 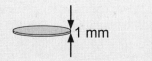 1 mm　　1 cm

4. Draw a line to match the object to the best unit to measure it.

   a) length of an ant　　　　　　m　　　　　b) height of a person　　　　km

   　 length of a car　　　　　　mm　　　　　 distance to the North Pole　cm

   c) length of a book　　　　　 mm　　　　 d) height of a building　　　　km

   　 length of a long street　　 cm　　　　　 width of Lake Erie　　　　　cm

   　 width of a street　　　　　 m　　　　　　 length of a small snake　　 m

   　 thickness of a cell phone　 km　　　　　 thickness of a coin　　　　 mm

5. Circle the measurement that best fills the blank.

a) The thickness of a piece of construction paper is about _____.

    1 mm   1 cm   1 dm   1 m   1 km

b) Schools might close if more than _____ of snow fell overnight.

    50 cm   50 dm   50 m   50 km

c) An average adult bicycle is about _____ long.

    2 mm   2 cm   2 dm   2 m   2 km

d) It is a little more than _____ from Sudbury, ON, to Thunder Bay, ON.

    1000 mm   1000 cm   1000 dm   1000 m   1000 km

6. Eric says that these two doors are both 2 m tall. He says that the doors must be the same height. Measuring in in which unit would help Eric to avoid this mistake? Explain.

  _____

2 m

7. Which unit of measurement (mm, cm, dm, m, or km) would you use to record the length of the sides of the polygon?

a) small flower bed: _____

b) plane flight plan: _____

St. John's, NL

Montreal, QC

Halifax, NS

c) playground: _____

d) postage stamp: _____

CANADA
postage
timbre

8. Marla wants to use ribbon to decorate the sides of a gift box. She does not want the ribbon to overlap.

a) Measure the sides of the gift box to the closest centimetre. Add the side lengths.

  _____ cm + _____ cm + _____ cm + _____ cm = _____ cm

b) Measure the sides of the gift box in millimetres. Add the side lengths.

  _____ mm + _____ mm + _____ mm + _____ mm = _____ mm

c) Did you get the same total length of ribbon? _____

d) Which answer should Marla use to cut the ribbon? _____

  Which unit is better for Marla's problem? _____

9. Jake's classroom is exactly 5 m long.

   a) How many decimetres long is Jake's classroom? _____ dm

   b) How many centimetres long is Jake's classroom? _____ cm

   c) How many millimetres long is Jake's classroom? _____ mm

   d) Which unit (m, dm, cm, or mm) gives the simplest measurement? _____

10. Tasha's desk is exactly 120 cm long.

   a) How many decimetres long is Tasha's desk? _____ dm

   b) How many metres long, to the closest metre, is Tasha's desk? _____ m

   c) How many millimetres long is Tasha's desk? _____ mm

   d) Which unit (m, dm, cm, or mm) gives the simplest measurement? _____

11. A button is 2 mm thick.

   a) Write the thickness to the closest unit.

   i) _____ cm   ii) _____ dm   iii) _____ m

   b) Which unit gives the most information about the thickness of the button? Explain.

   _____

12. Kim's room is 3 m 75 cm long.

   a) How many metres long (to the closest metre) is Kim's room? _____

   b) How many centimetres long is Kim's room? _____

   c) Write the measurements in the table in centimetres and in metres to the closest metre.

Object	Length	Length in cm	Length in m
bed	1 m 90 cm		
shelf	85 cm		
desk	1 m 23 cm		

   d) Add the lengths of the objects in part c) in metres. Do you think the objects will fit along the length of Kim's room?

   e) Add the lengths of the objects in part c) in centimetres. Do you think the objects will fit along the length of Kim's room?

   f) Which unit, metres or centimetres, is better to decide if the objects will fit in Kim's room? Explain.

ME4-7 Mass

Mass is the amount of matter in an object. The heavier the object, the greater its mass.

1. Match each object in the top row to an object with a similar mass in the bottom row.

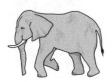   

The mass of small objects is measured in **grams**. We write 1 **g** for 1 gram.

A large paper clip weighs about 1 gram.

A tennis ball weighs about 50 g. A small potato weighs about 100 g.

2. Circle the objects that have a mass of 100 g or more. Draw an ✕ on objects that have a mass less than 50 g.

3. What is the mass of the object?

a)

mass of orange:

about _____ g

b)

mass of fish:

about _____ g

c)

mass of 1 pair of scissors:

about _____ g

4. Estimate the mass of the object in grams. Use a scale to measure the mass.

a) a cookie

Estimate: _____   Measure: _____

b) an apple

Estimate: _____   Measure: _____

c) a shoe

Estimate: _____   Measure: _____

d) a pencil

Estimate: _____   Measure: _____

We measure the mass of larger objects in **kilograms** (**kg**).

A tall thin carton of orange juice has a mass of 1 kg.

1 kg = 1000 g

5. Circle the correct mass for the item.

a)

2 g or 2 kg

b)

15 g or 15 kg

c)

35 g or 35 kg

d)

270 g or 270 kg

6. Circle the unit that is better for measuring the mass of the item.

a) pencil

g or kg

b) desk

g or kg

c) your backpack

g or kg

d) student

g or kg

e) moose

g or kg

f) tiny bird

g or kg

g) slice of cheese

g or kg

h) car

g or kg

7. Estimate the mass of the object in kilograms. Measure the mass to the nearest kilogram.

a) a backpack

Estimate: _____   Measure: _____

b) a large bottle of water

Estimate: _____   Measure: _____

c) a pile of books

Estimate: _____   Measure: _____

d) a basketball

Estimate: _____   Measure: _____

8. Cross out the objects that weigh more than 1 kg. Circle the objects that weigh between 1 g and 1 kg.

9. a) A small melon weighs 675 g. Another small melon weighs 508 g. Do these melons together weigh more than 1 kg? Explain.

b) A watermelon weighs 3764 g. Another watermelon weighs 4890 g. Do the two watermelons together weigh more than 10 kg? Explain.

ME4-8 Comparing Units of Mass

> **REMINDER** ▶ 1 kilogram = 1000 grams   1 kg = 1000 g

1. Fill in the table.

kg	1	2	3	4	5	6	7	8
g	*1000*							

2. How many whole kilograms are in the measurement?

   a) 3648 g _3 kg_   b) 8721 g _____   c) 10 000 g _____   d) 979 g _____

3. a) What is lighter, 999 g or 1 kg? How do you know? _____

   _____

   b) Ronin thinks that 6 kg is lighter than 225 g because 6 is less than 225. Is he correct?

   Explain. _____

4. Underline the number of whole kilograms in the measurement in grams. Circle the
   heavier measurement.

   a) <u>5</u>000 g (7 kg)   b) 8300 g   95 kg   c) 2567 g   15 kg

   d) 2222 g   2 kg   e) 60 kg   6200 g   f) 7 kg   4503 g

5. Use the table in Question 1.

   a) Write a measurement in grams that is between 5 kg and 6 kg. _____

   b) Write a measurement in kilograms that is between 3790 g and 4258 g. _____

6. Convert the measurement in grams to a mixed measurement.

   a) 5130 g = __5__ kg __130__ g   b) 5217 g = _____ kg _____ g

   c) 4367 g = _____ kg _____ g   d) 4081 g = _____ kg _____ g

   e) 7006 g = _____ kg _____ g   f) 9300 g = _____ kg _____ g

7. Order the babies from lightest to heaviest.

   Abella: 3547 g   Matt: 4 kg   Emma: 4 kg 45 g   Marko: 3 kg 206 g

   _____

> **BONUS** ▶ A letter carrier is carrying 300 letters in his bag. Each letter has a mass of about 10 g.
>
>   What is the total mass of the letters in kilograms? _____

We measure the mass of very small objects in **milligrams**. Write 1 **mg** for 1 milligram.

Here are some masses in milligrams:

small ant: about 1 mg   grain of sand: about 10 mg   5-dollar bill: 930 mg

8. Will you use grams or milligrams to measure the mass?

   a) grain of rice

   mg   g

   b) pebble

   mg   g

   c) small feather

   mg   g

We use milligrams when we need to be precise. Doctors use milligrams for medications.

9. Circle the measurement that fills the blank best.

   a) Each pill contains _____ of vitamin C.   500 mg   500 g

   b) A 2-dollar coin weighs about _____.   7 mg   7 g

   c) A cup can hold _____ of flour.   125 mg   125 g

   d) A drop of rain weighs about _____.   150 mg   150 g

   e) A grain of sand weighs about _____.   5 mg   5 kg

   f) A mug of hot tea weighs about _____.   600 g   600 kg

   g) A chocolate chip weighs about _____.   400 mg   400 g   400 kg

   h) A male grizzly bear can weigh up to _____.   770 mg   770 g   770 kg

10. Choose two parts in Question 9 and explain how you chose your answer.

   _____

   _____

   _____

11. Tomato and eggplant seeds weigh 3 mg each. Zucchini seeds weigh 120 mg each.
    David bought 100 tomato seeds, 100 eggplant seeds, and 10 zucchini seeds. How much
    did his seeds weigh altogether? Do they weigh more than 1 g? More than 10 g? Explain.

12. The table shows the masses of some Antarctic birds.

    a) Order the birds from heaviest to lightest.

    b) Use the information in the table to create a word problem.

    c) Solve the problem you created in part b).

Antarctic Bird	Mass
Adélie penguin	6 kg 500 g
Emperor penguin	45 kg
Cape petrel	550 g
Giant Antarctic petrel	5 kg
Snow petrel	300 g
Wandering albatross	9900 g

We can use circles to sort objects by their properties.
Objects inside a circle have the property, and objects outside the circle do not.

Use these shapes for Questions 1, 2, and 3.

1. Put the letters from each shape inside or outside the circle.

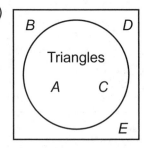 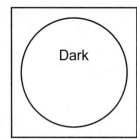 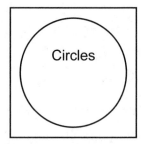

Objects can be in more than one circle at the same time.
Objects in the overlapping region share the properties of both circles or ovals.

2. a) Shade the region that is **inside** both ovals.
       Put the correct letter in that area.

    b) Shade the region that is **outside** both ovals.
       Put the correct letters in that area.

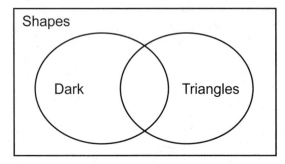 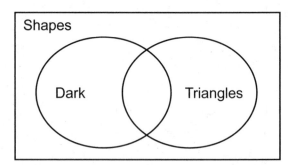

3. Complete the Venn diagram.

    a)

    b)

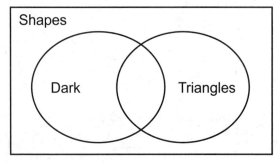 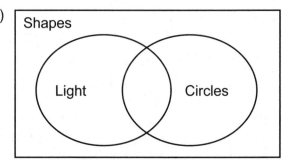

4. Complete the Venn diagram.

A. bat **B.** dog **C.** owl **D.** cat **E.** mosquito **F.** flamingo **G.** sparrow **H.** bee

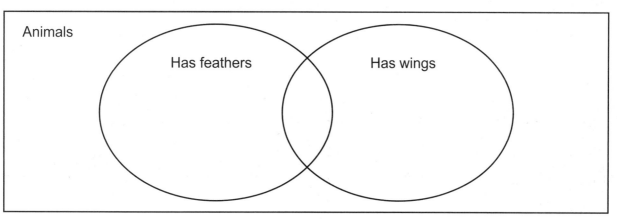

One part of the Venn diagram is empty. Explain what that means. _____

_____

5. Complete the Venn diagram.

a) **A.** rice   **B.** hat   **C.** sit   **D.** rat

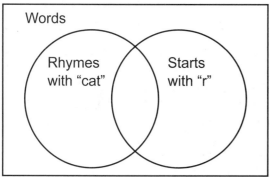

b) **A.** human   **B.** chair   **C.** fish   **D.** worm

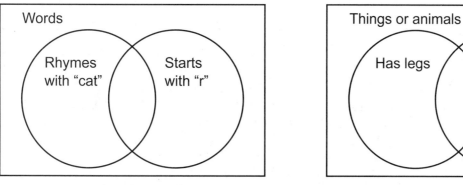

c) **A.** cat   **B.** listen   **C.** watch   **D.** fly

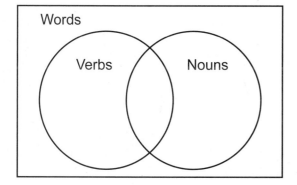

d) **A.** P.E.I.   **B.** Asia   **C.** Boston   **D.** Canada

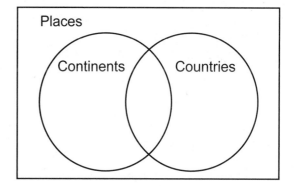

1. Fill in the missing labels.

a)

Pens	*Not* ___ *pens* ___

b)

Blue	
___ ___	

c)

	Pens	___ ___
Blue		
___ ___		

d)

		Not square
___		
___ Not polygons		

2. Write the kind of number that goes in each region. Then write two numbers in each region.

a)

	Less than 5	Not less than 5
Even	*less than 5* ___ and ___ *even* ___ ___ 2, 4 ___	*not less than 5* ___ and ___ ___ 8, ___
Not even	___ and ___ *not even* ___ ___ 1, ___	___ and ___ ___

b)

	Greater than 11	Not greater than 11
Odd	___ and ___ ___	___ and ___ ___
Not odd	___ and ___ *not odd* ___ ___ 12, ___	___ and ___ ___

3. Cross out the two terms in each region that should **not** be there.

a)

	Less than 15	Not less than 15
Odd	5, ~~9~~ 11, ~~16~~	17, 19, 20, 100
Not odd	4, 6, 7, 23	14, 25, 30, 60

b)

	Multiple of 5	Not multiple of 5
Less than 50	5, 18, 20, 94	25, 28, 37, 60
Not less than 50	45, 60, 75, 82	35, 60, 61, 99

c)

	Four sides	Not four sides
Striped		
Not striped		

BONUS ▶

	Rhymes with "made"	Does not rhyme with "made"
4 letters	said wade paid trade	late weight aid make
Not 4 letters	grade wait jade played	strain raid fade had

G4-3 Polygons

All 2-D (flat) shapes have **sides** (or edges) and **vertices** (the corners where the sides meet).

vertices → ← sides

1. Count the number of sides and vertices in the shape. Put a check mark on each side and circle each vertex as you count.

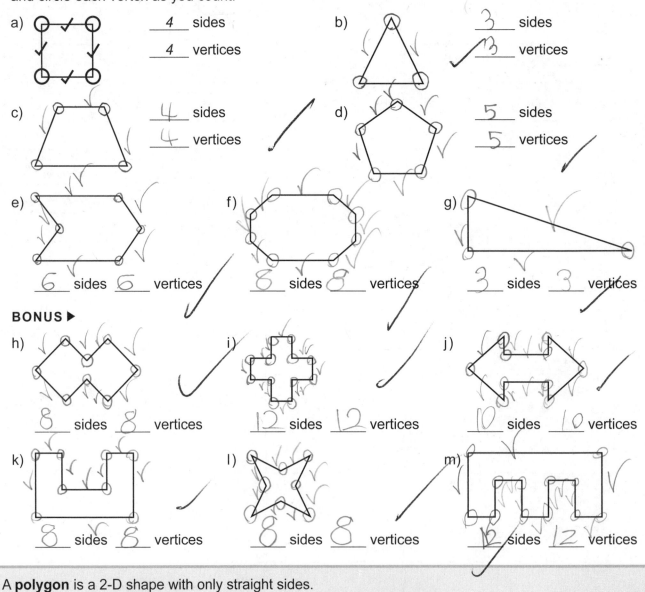

a) _4_ sides
   _4_ vertices

b) _3_ sides
   _3_ vertices

c) _4_ sides
   _4_ vertices

d) _5_ sides
   _5_ vertices

e) _6_ sides _6_ vertices

f) _8_ sides _8_ vertices

g) _3_ sides _3_ vertices

BONUS ▶

h) _8_ sides _8_ vertices

i) _12_ sides _12_ vertices

j) _10_ sides _10_ vertices

k) _8_ sides _8_ vertices

l) _8_ sides _8_ vertices

m) _12_ sides _12_ vertices

A **polygon** is a 2-D shape with only straight sides.

2. These shapes have both straight and curved sides. Fill in the missing numbers.

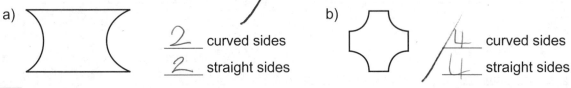

a) _2_ curved sides
   _2_ straight sides

b) _4_ curved sides
   _4_ straight sides

c) Are these shapes polygons? Explain.

Polygons are named according to how many sides they have.

3 sides	triangle		5 sides	pentagon
4 sides	quadrilateral		6 sides	hexagon

3. Count the sides. Then name the shape.

a) 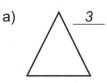 _3_ sides

triangle

b) _6_ sides

hexagon

c) _5_ sides

Pentagon

d) _4_ sides

quadrilateral

4. Find the number of sides and complete the chart.

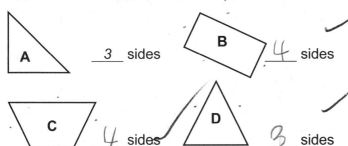

A _3_ sides

B _4_ sides

C _4_ sides

D _3_ sides

Name	Shapes
Triangle	A, D
Quadrilateral	BC

5. Complete the chart. Find as many shapes as you can for each shape name.

Name	Shapes
Triangle	A
Quadrilateral	FBG
Pentagon	DC
Hexagon	HE

6. Use a ruler. Draw a polygon with …

a) 3 sides   b) 4 sides

c) 5 sides   d) 6 sides

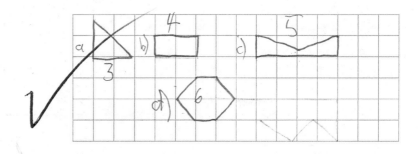

7. a) Count the vertices in the polygons you drew above. What do you notice?

b) Can you draw a polygon in which the number of sides does not equal the number of vertices?

G4-4 Benchmark Angles

An **angle** is formed when two rays share the same endpoint.

angles

Sometimes angles are shown without arrows.

1. Circle the pictures that show angles.

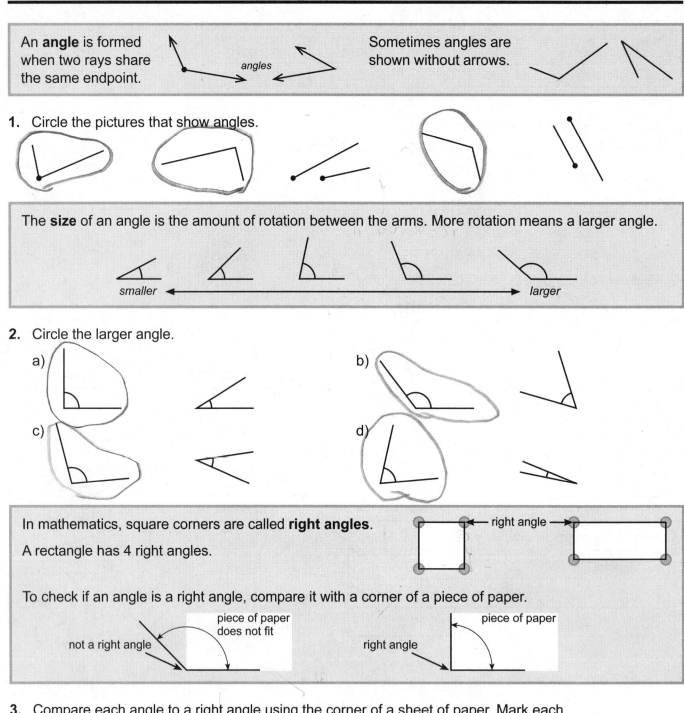

The **size** of an angle is the amount of rotation between the arms. More rotation means a larger angle.

smaller ⟵————————————⟶ *larger*

2. Circle the larger angle.

a)

b)

c)

d)

In mathematics, square corners are called **right angles**.

A rectangle has 4 right angles.

right angle

To check if an angle is a right angle, compare it with a corner of a piece of paper.

piece of paper does not fit
not a right angle

piece of paper
right angle

3. Compare each angle to a right angle using the corner of a sheet of paper. Mark each angle as less than a right angle, equal to a right angle, or greater than a right angle.

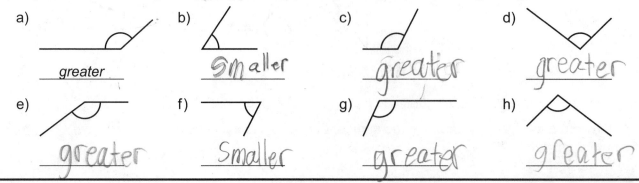

a) _greater_

b) _smaller_

c) _greater_

d) _greater_

e) _greater_

f) _smaller_

g) _greater_

h) _greater_

4. Circle the right angles. Check your answers with the corner of a piece of paper.

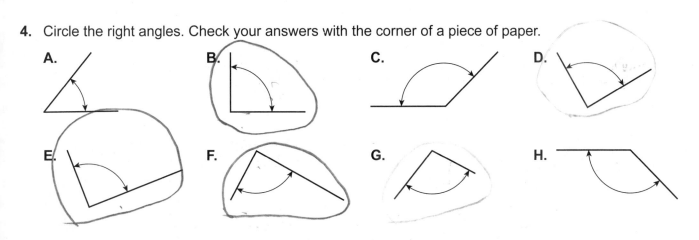

A.   B.   C.   D.

E.   F.   G.   H.

5. Place each angle from Question 4 in the Venn diagram.

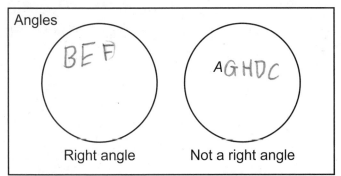

Angles

BEF

AGHDC

Right angle   Not a right angle

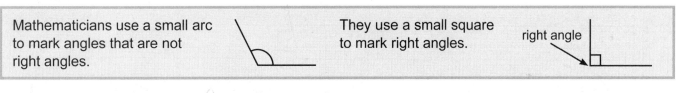

Mathematicians use a small arc to mark angles that are not right angles.

They use a small square to mark right angles.

right angle

6. Mark all right angles with a small square. Does the shape have right angles?

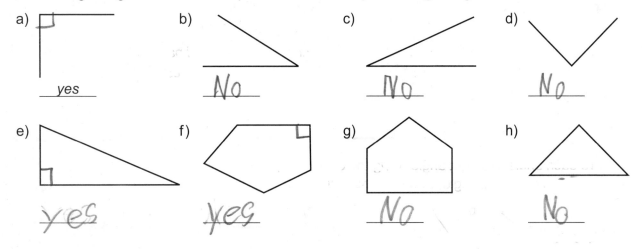

a)   _____yes_____

b)   _____No_____

c)   _____No_____

d)   _____No_____

e)   _____yes_____

f)   _____yes_____

g)   _____No_____

h)   _____No_____

7. Circle the shape that has no right angle.

You can use the corner of a folded piece of paper
to compare any angle to a 45 degree angle.

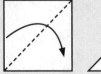

This angle is greater than a 45 degree angle.

8. Use the corner of a folded piece of paper to compare each angle to a 45 degree angle.
   Then write in the blanks "less than 45," "equal to 45," or "greater than 45."

A.

_____

B.

_____

C.

_____

D.

_____

E.

_____

F.

_____

G.

_____

H.

_____

9. Place each angle from Question 8 in the Venn diagram.

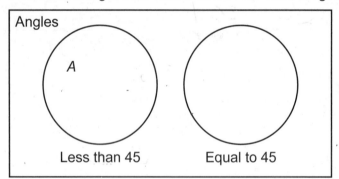

Angles

A

Less than 45   Equal to 45

BONUS ▶ Place these angles in the Venn diagram.

I.   J.   K.   L.   M.   N.

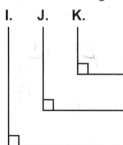   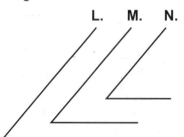

G4-5 Regular and Irregular Polygons

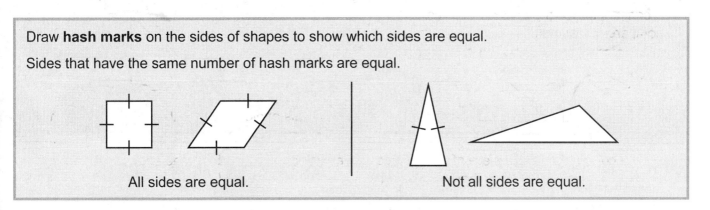

Draw **hash marks** on the sides of shapes to show which sides are equal.

Sides that have the same number of hash marks are equal.

All sides are equal.   Not all sides are equal.

1. Write "equal" under the shapes that have all sides equal. Write "not equal" under all
   the other shapes.

a)   b)   c)

unequal   *unequal*   *u equal*

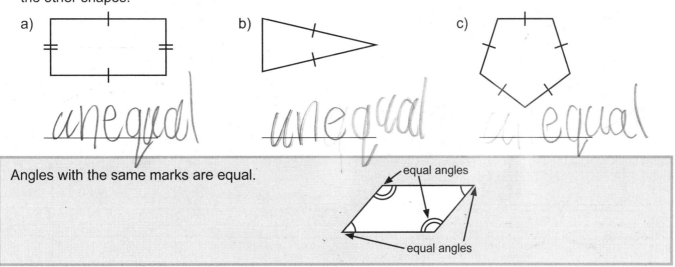

Angles with the same marks are equal.

equal angles

equal angles

2. Write "equal" under the shapes that have all angles equal. Write "not equal" under all
   the other shapes.

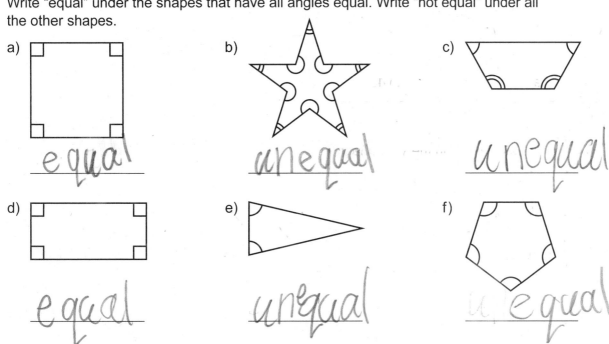

a)   b)   c)

equal   *unequal*   *unequal*

d)   e)   f)

equal   *unequal*   *u equal*

Regular polygons have all sides and all angles equal.

All other polygons are irregular.

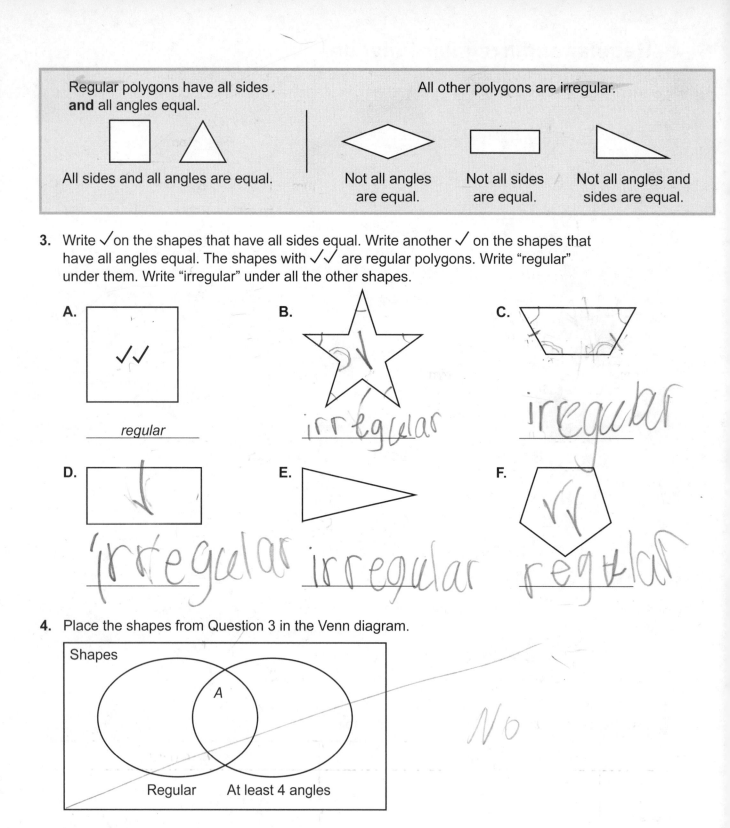

All sides and all angles are equal.

Not all angles are equal.

Not all sides are equal.

Not all angles and sides are equal.

3. Write ✓ on the shapes that have all sides equal. Write another ✓ on the shapes that have all angles equal. The shapes with ✓✓ are regular polygons. Write "regular" under them. Write "irregular" under all the other shapes.

A.
✓✓

regular

B.
irregular

C.
irregular

D.
irregular

E.
irregular

F.
regular

4. Place the shapes from Question 3 in the Venn diagram.

Shapes

A

Regular   At least 4 angles

No

BONUS ▶ Where would you put this shape in the Venn diagram?

5. Measure the sides of each shape. Draw hash marks to show which sides are equal.
Is the shape regular or irregular?

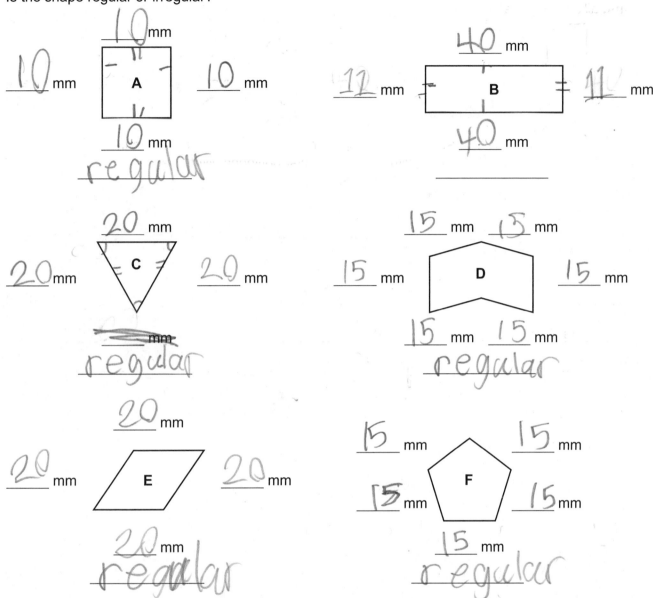

A: 10 mm (top), 10 mm (left), 10 mm (right), 10 mm (bottom) — regular

B: 40 mm (top), 11 mm (left), 11 mm (right), 40 mm (bottom)

C: 20 mm (top), 20 mm (left), 20 mm (right), ___ mm — regular

D: 15 mm, 15 mm, 15 mm (left), 15 mm (right), 15 mm, 15 mm — regular

E: 20 mm (top), 20 mm (left), 20 mm (right), 20 mm (bottom) — regular

F: 15 mm, 15 mm, 15 mm, 15 mm, 15 mm — regular

6. Place the shapes from Question 5 in the Carroll diagram.

	Regular	Not regular
4 sides		NO
Not 4 sides		

G4-6 Parallel Sides

Parallel sides are like straight railroad tracks: they go in the same direction and are always the same distance apart.

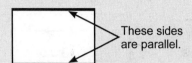 These sides are parallel.

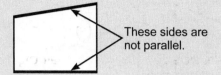 These sides are not parallel.

1. Are the thicker sides parallel?

a)

_____yes_____

b)

yes

c)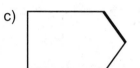

NO

d)

No

e)

No

f)

yes

g)

yes

h)

yes

2. The picture shows two parallel sides. Join the dots to make a quadrilateral.

a)

b)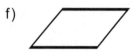

c)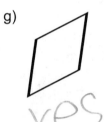

d)

e)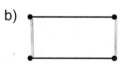

f)

g)

h)

i)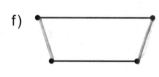

Use arrows to mark parallel sides.

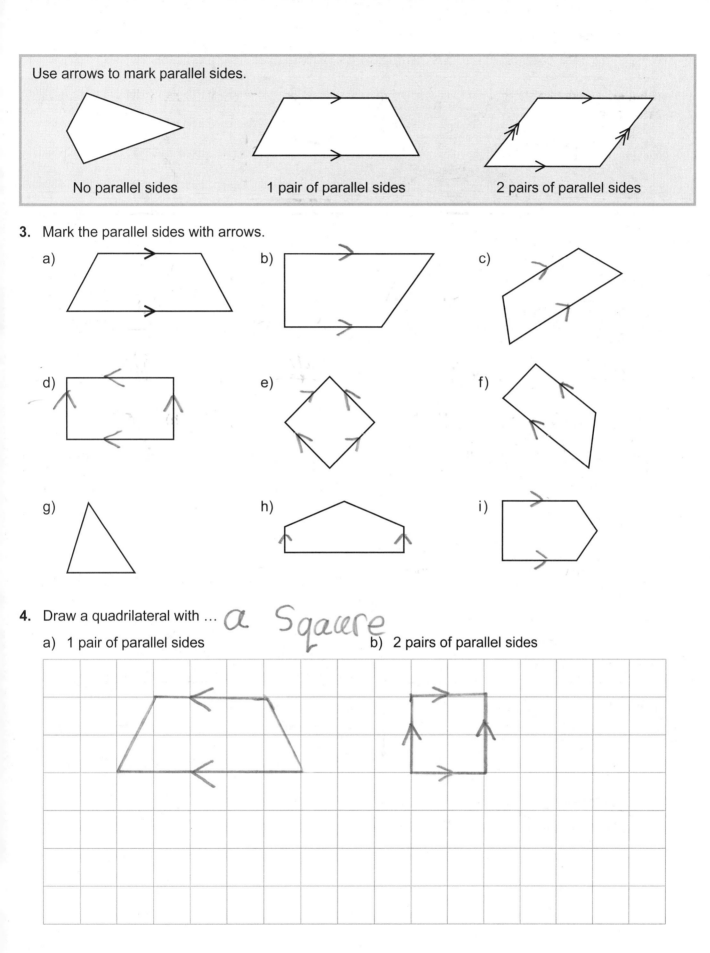

No parallel sides   1 pair of parallel sides   2 pairs of parallel sides

3. Mark the parallel sides with arrows.

a)

b)

c)

d)

e)

f)

g)

h)

i)

4. Draw a quadrilateral with ... *a Sqaure*

a) 1 pair of parallel sides   b) 2 pairs of parallel sides

5. a) Mark the parallel sides with arrows. Write how many pairs of sides are parallel.

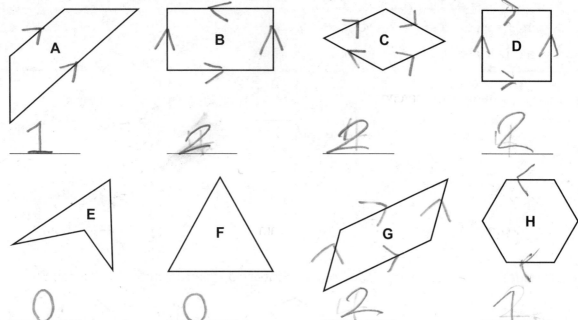

A 1

B 2

C 2

D 2

E 0

F 0

G 2

H 1

b) Complete the Venn diagram for the shapes in part a).

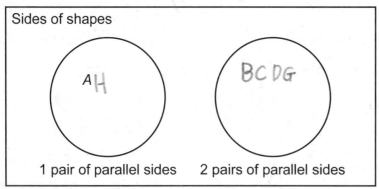

Sides of shapes

A H — 1 pair of parallel sides

BC DG — 2 pairs of parallel sides

Parallel sides must be straight.

6. Are the thicker sides parallel?

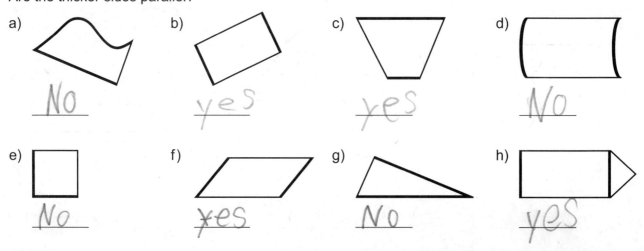

a) No

b) yes

c) yes

d) No

e) No

f) yes

g) No

h) yes

A **parallelogram** is a quadrilateral with two pairs of parallel sides.

A **trapezoid** is a quadrilateral with only one pair of parallel sides.

1. Write ✓ beside the name that matches the shape.

a)

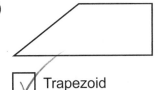

☑ Trapezoid

☐ Parallelogram

b)

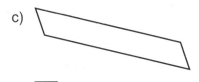

☑ Trapezoid

☐ Parallelogram

c)

☐ Trapezoid

☑ Parallelogram

2. Mark parallel sides with arrows. Label the shape as "trapezoid," "parallelogram," or "neither."

a)

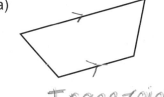

Trapezoid ✓

b)

Parallelogram ✓

c)

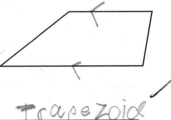

Trapezoid

d)

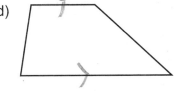

Trapezoid ✓

e)

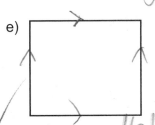

parallelogram

f)

trapezoid

g)

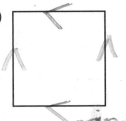

paralllogram

h)

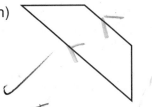

Trapezoid

i)

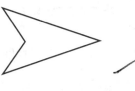

nothing

j)

nothing

k)

Nothing

l)

parallgram

3. Does the name match the shape? Write ✓ or ✗.

a)

☑ Rectangle
☑ Parallelogram

b)

☒ Rectangle
☒ Parallelogram

c)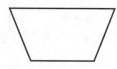

☒ Rectangle
☑ Parallelogram

d)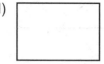

☑ Rectangle
☑ Parallelogram

e)

☑ Rectangle
☑ Parallelogram

f)

☑ Rectangle
☑ Parallelogram

4. Does the name match the shape? Write ✓ or ✗.

a)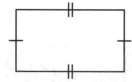

☒ Rhombus
☑ Parallelogram

b)

☒ Rhombus
☒ Parallelogram

c)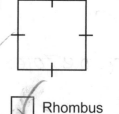

☑ Rhombus
☑ Parallelogram

d)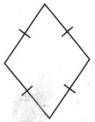

☒ Rhombus
☒ Parallelogram

e)

☒ Rhombus
☒ Parallelogram

f)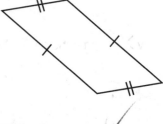

☒ Rhombus
☒ Parallelogram

Geometry 4-7

G4-8 Congruent Shapes

Karen places shapes one on top of the other. She tries to make the shapes match.

If they match exactly, the shapes are **congruent**.

Congruent shapes have the same size and shape.

Congruent shapes  | Not congruent shapes

1. Are the shapes congruent? Write "yes" or "no."

a)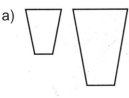
_____no_____

b)
yes

c)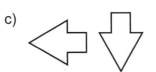
yes

d)
no

e)
no

f)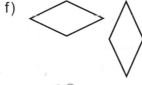
yes

g)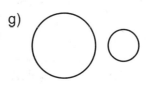
no

h)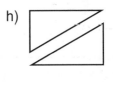
yes

2. Circle the two congruent shapes.

a)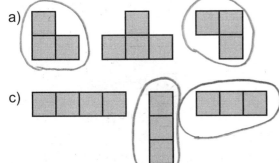

b)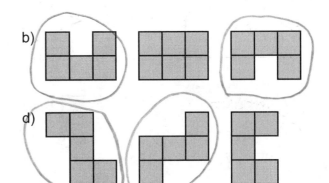

c)

d)

3. Draw ✕ on the shape that is not congruent to the other two.

a)

b)

c)

d)

Geometry 4-8

4. Find the dark shape that is congruent to the light shape. Fill in the letter of the dark shape. You may need to use a ruler.

A. **B.** **C.** **D.** **E.** **F.**

a) B

b) E

c) A

d) F

e) C

f) D

5. Circle the two shapes that are congruent.

a)

b)

c)

BONUS ▶

d)

e)

6. Draw a shape congruent to the shaded shape.

a)

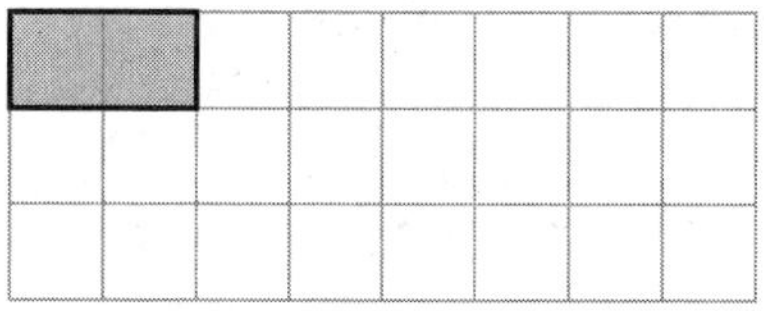

b)

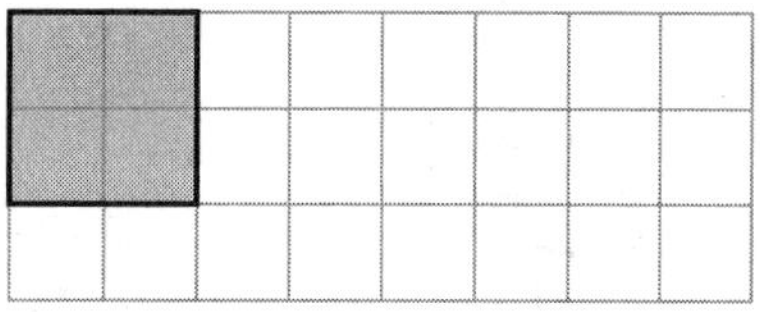

c)

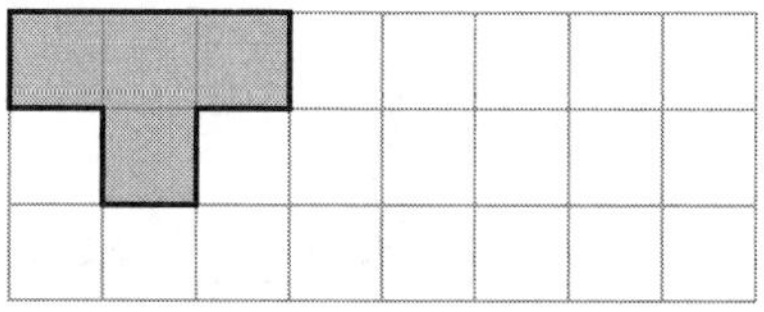

d)

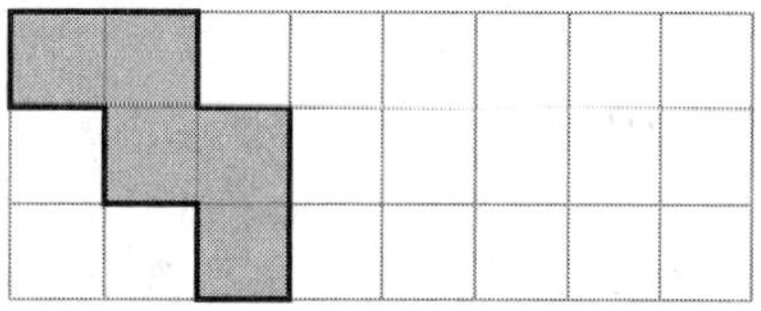

7. Draw a polygon of the given type that is not congruent to the shaded shape.

a) a square

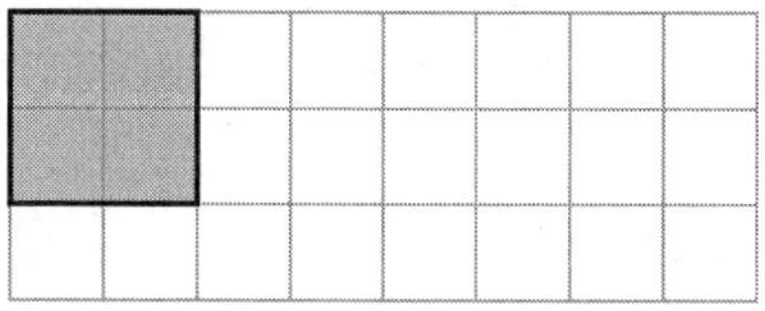

b) a trapezoid

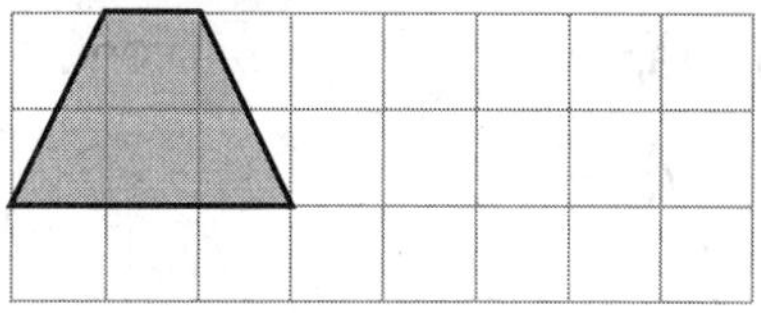

c) a rectangle

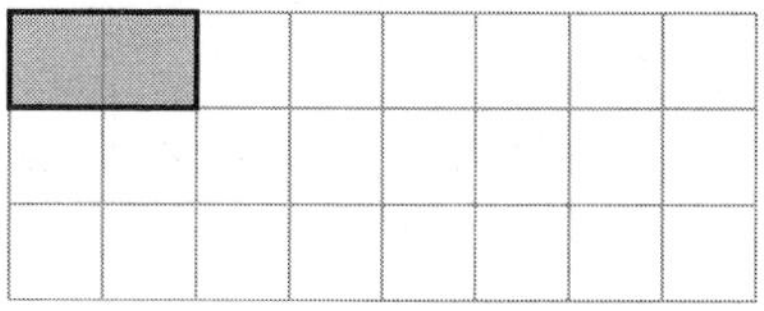

d) a triangle

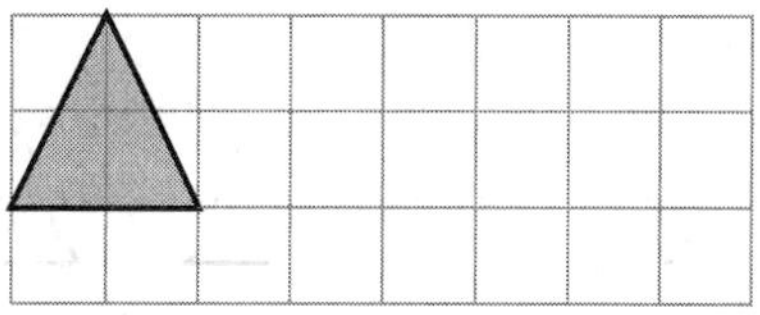

8. Draw two triangles that are not congruent.

9. Are the shapes congruent? Explain.

a)

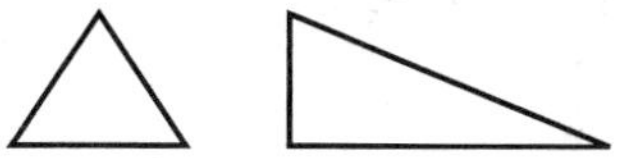

_____

_____

_____

_____

b)

_____

_____

_____

_____

G4-9 Symmetry

1. Ira draws a line to break the shape into two parts. Are the parts of the shape congruent?

a)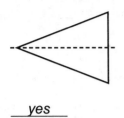

yes

b)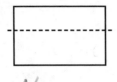

No

c)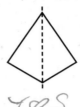

Yes

d)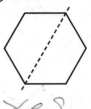

Yes

When you can fold a shape in half so that the parts match exactly, the fold is called a **line of symmetry**.

Parts match exactly.

fold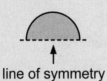

line of symmetry

Parts do not match.

fold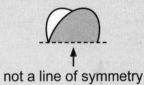

not a line of symmetry

2. Is the dashed line a line of symmetry?

a)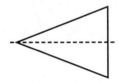

yes

b)

Yes

c)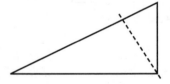

No

d)

Yes

e)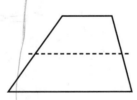

No

f)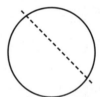

No

g)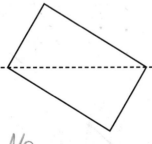

No

h)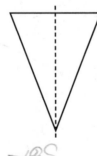

Yes

i)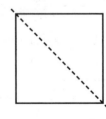

Yes

3. Use a ruler. Draw a line of symmetry.

a)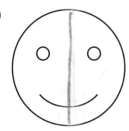

b)

c)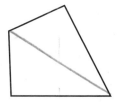

d)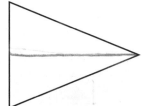

e)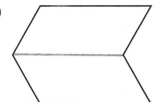

f)

g)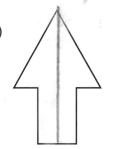

h)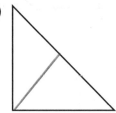

i)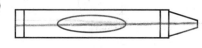

j)

k)

l)

4. Draw two lines of symmetry.

a)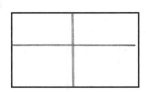

b)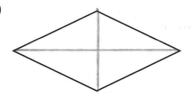

c)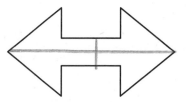

BONUS ▶ Draw four lines of symmetry.

a)

b)

c)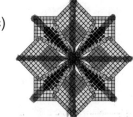

5. The dashed line is the line of symmetry. Draw the missing part of the picture. Use a ruler.

a)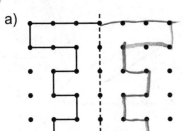

b)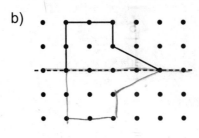

c)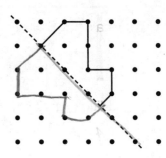

6. Sketch the missing part of the picture so that it has a line of symmetry. Hint: First draw the line of symmetry.

a)

b)

c)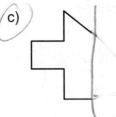

7. Sketch the missing part of the picture so that it has two lines of symmetry. Draw both lines of symmetry.

a)

b)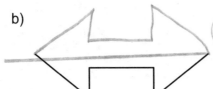

c)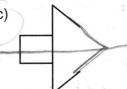

BONUS ▶ Sketch the missing parts. Then draw another line of symmetry.

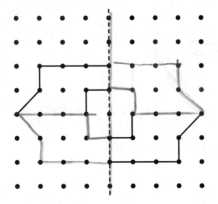

8. Draw a picture that has a line of symmetry in the given direction.

a) horizontal   b) vertical   c) diagonal

9. Draw a figure with more than one line of symmetry. How many lines of symmetry does it have? What lines of symmetry are they?

         Geometry 4-9

PA4-1 Multiplication and Addition I

Multiplying is a short way of adding: $4 \times 5 = \underbrace{5 + 5 + 5 + 5}$

add 5 four times

1. Write an addition for each multiplication.

   a) $3 \times 4 = 4 + 4 + 4$ b) $2 \times 8 =$ c) $5 \times 6 =$

   d) $4 \times 2 =$ e) $3 \times 5 =$ f) $6 \times 3 =$

   g) $5 \times 7 =$ h) $2 \times 1 =$ i) $1 \times 8 =$

2. Write a multiplication for each addition.

   a) $4 + 4 + 4 = 3 \times 4$ b) $5 + 5 + 5 =$ c) $4 + 4 =$

   d) $2 + 2 + 2 =$ e) $9 + 9 + 9 + 9 =$ f) $1 + 1 + 1 =$

   g) $6 + 6 + 6 + 6 + 6 =$ h) $8 + 8 + 8 + 8 + 8 =$ i) $3 + 3 + 3 + 3 =$

3. Write an addition and a multiplication for each picture.

   a) 3 boxes; 2 pencils in each box

   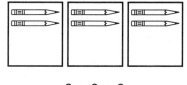

   $\underline{\qquad 2 + 2 + 2 \qquad}$

   $\underline{\qquad 3 \times 2 \qquad}$

   b) 3 boxes; 4 pencils in each box

   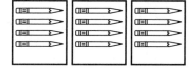

   $\underline{\hspace{4cm}}$

   $\underline{\hspace{4cm}}$

   c) 4 boxes; 3 pencils in each box

   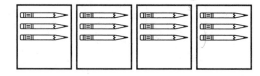

   $\underline{\hspace{4cm}}$

   $\underline{\hspace{4cm}}$

   d) 2 boxes; 5 pencils in each box

   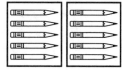

   $\underline{\hspace{4cm}}$

   $\underline{\hspace{4cm}}$

   e) 5 boxes; 3 pencils in each box

   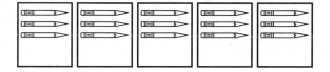

   $\underline{\hspace{4cm}}$

   $\underline{\hspace{4cm}}$

   f) 4 boxes; 2 pencils in each box

   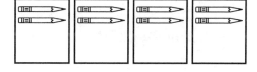

   $\underline{\hspace{4cm}}$

   $\underline{\hspace{4cm}}$

4. Add the numbers. Write your subtotals in the boxes provided.

Example: $4 + 5 + 7 =$ _____ $\xrightarrow[\text{(= 9)}]{\text{add } 4 + 5}$ $4 + 5 + 7 =$ _____ $\xrightarrow[\text{(= 16)}]{\text{add } 9 + 7}$ $4 + 5 + 7 =$ __16__

a) $2 + 3 + 5 =$ _____

b) $3 + 3 + 7 =$ _____

c) $5 + 4 + 3 =$ _____

d) $6 + 4 + 2 =$ _____

e) $8 + 3 + 4 =$ _____

f) $9 + 1 + 6 =$ _____

g) $4 + 3 + 3 + 2 =$ _____

h) $4 + 5 + 5 + 3 =$ _____

i) $6 + 7 + 3 + 5 =$ _____

5. Write an addition for each picture. Add to find out how many apples there are altogether. Check your answer by counting the apples.

a) 3 boxes; 3 apples in each box

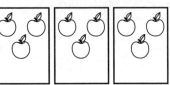

_____

b) 4 boxes; 2 apples in each box

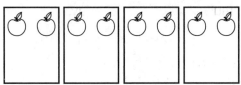

_____

c) 4 boxes; 4 apples in each box

_____

d) 3 boxes; 5 apples in each box

_____

6. Draw a picture, and write an addition and a multiplication for your picture.

a) 3 vans
   7 people in each van

b) 4 bags
   5 books in each bag

c) 6 boxes
   4 pens in each box

d) 5 boats
   4 campers in each boat

7. Write an addition and a multiplication for each situation.

a) 6 plates
   8 crackers on each plate

b) 7 bags
   3 gifts in each bag

c) 4 baskets
   7 bananas in each basket

PA4-2 Arrays

In the **array** below, there are 3 **rows** of dots. There are 5 dots **in each row**.

   5
     10   *Marcel counts the dots*
     15   *by skip counting by 5s.*

Marcel writes a multiplication equation for the array: **3 × 5 = 15** (3 rows of 5 dots is 15 dots).

1. How many rows are there? How many dots in each row?
   Write a multiplication equation for the array.

   a)

   __3__ rows

   __4__ dots in each row

   ____3 × 4 = 12____

   b)

   _____ rows

   _____ dots in each row

   _____

   c)

   _____ rows

   _____ dots in each row

   _____

2. Write a multiplication for the array.

   a)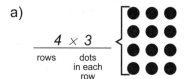

   __4 × 3__
   rows   dots
        in each
         row

   b)

   _____

   c)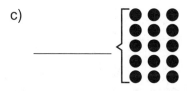

   _____

   d)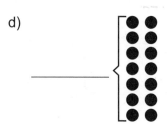

   _____

3. Draw an array for the multiplication.

   a) 5 × 5   b) 3 × 5   c) 2 × 4   d) 4 × 3   e) 1 × 6   f) 2 × 5

4. Draw an array and write a multiplication equation to find each answer.

   a) On a bus, 4 people can sit in a row. There are 6 rows of seats on the bus.
      How many people can ride on the bus?

   b) In a garden, there are 3 rows of plants. There are 5 plants in each row.
      How many plants are there altogether?

   c) Jenny planted 8 seeds in each row. There are 4 rows of seeds.
      How many seeds did Jenny plant?

We can group the dots in this array: by rows: or by columns:

$$3 \times 4 = 12 \qquad 4 \times 3 = 12$$

5. Group the dots by rows and then by columns. Write two multiplication equations.

a)

_____   _____

b)

_____   _____

c)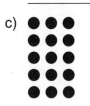

_____   _____

d)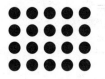

_____   _____

6. Fill in the blanks.

a) 2 rows of 5 dots each is the same as _____ columns of _____ dots each, so $2 \times 5 = $ _____ $\times$ _____.

b) 3 rows of 7 dots each is the same as _____ columns of _____ dots each, so $3 \times 7 = $ _____ $\times$ _____.

c) 5 rows of 8 dots each is the same as _____

_____ , so $5 \times 8 = $ _____ .

7. a) The picture shows _____ rows of _____ dots each.

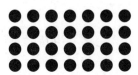

b) Now turn the page sideways.

After turning the page sideways, the picture shows _____ rows of _____ dots each.

c) Did turning the page change the number of dots in the picture? _____

d) Write an equation that shows your answer to part c). _____ $\times$ _____ = _____ $\times$ _____

8. Draw a picture to show that $2 \times 7 = 7 \times 2$.

Patterns and Algebra 4-2

PA4-3 Multiplying by Skip Counting

Randi finds the **3 × 5** by skip counting on a number line.

She counts off three 5s:

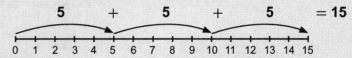

$$5 + 5 + 5 = 15$$

From the picture, Randi can see that **3 × 5 = 15**.

1. Show how to find the answer by skip counting.
   Use arrows like the ones in Randi's picture.

   a) $4 \times 3 =$

   b) $7 \times 2 =$

   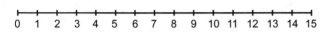 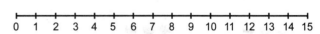

2. Use the number line to skip count by 4s, 6s, and 7s. Fill in the boxes as you count.

   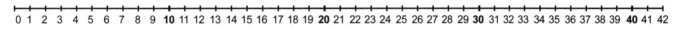

   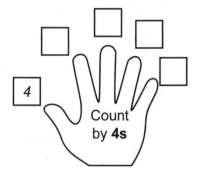 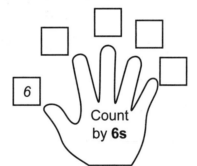 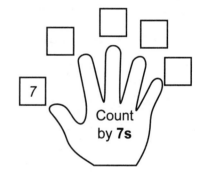

3. Multiply by skip counting on your fingers. Use the hands from Question 2 to help.

       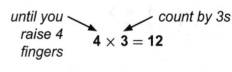

   a) $4 \times 5 =$ b) $5 \times 2 =$ c) $4 \times 4 =$ d) $2 \times 6 =$ e) $7 \times 1 =$

   f) $3 \times 7 =$ g) $3 \times 3 =$ h) $6 \times 1 =$ i) $2 \times 7 =$ j) $5 \times 5 =$

4. Find the number of items by skip counting. Write a multiplication for each picture.

   a)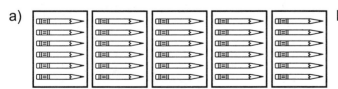

   b)

Patterns and Algebra 4-3

PA4-4 Patterns in Times Tables

1. a) Shade the **multiples** of 5 (the numbers you say when counting by 5s starting from 0).

   b) What patterns can you see in the positions of the multiples of 5? Use the words "rows," "columns," or "diagonals" in your answer.

   _____

   _____

   _____

   _____

   _____

   _____

1	2	3	4	5	6	7	8	9	10
11	12	13	14	15	16	17	18	19	20
21	22	23	24	25	26	27	28	29	30
31	32	33	34	35	36	37	38	39	40
41	42	43	44	45	46	47	48	49	50
51	52	53	54	55	56	57	58	59	60
61	62	63	64	65	66	67	68	69	70
71	72	73	74	75	76	77	78	79	80
81	82	83	84	85	86	87	88	89	90
91	92	93	94	95	96	97	98	99	100

2. What do you notice about the ones digits?

   _____

3. How can you tell whether a number between 1 and 100 is a multiple of 5 without counting up?

   _____

4. Circle the multiples of 5.

   a) 8   16   45   27   60   62   90   85   11   25   50   37

   b) 203   205   217   225   385   426   589   755   931

5. a) Pick two multiples of 5 smaller than 50. Add them. _____ + _____ = _____

   b) Is your answer to part a) a multiple of 5? _____

   c) Will this always be true? Explain.

   _____

   _____

6. a) Shade the multiples of 2.

b) What patterns can you see in the positions of the multiples of 2? Use the words "rows," "columns," or "diagonals" in your answer.

_____

_____

_____

_____

_____

1	2	3	4	5	6	7	8	9	10
11	12	13	14	15	16	17	18	19	20
21	22	23	24	25	26	27	28	29	30
31	32	33	34	35	36	37	38	39	40
41	42	43	44	45	46	47	48	49	50
51	52	53	54	55	56	57	58	59	60
61	62	63	64	65	66	67	68	69	70
71	72	73	74	75	76	77	78	79	80
81	82	83	84	85	86	87	88	89	90
91	92	93	94	95	96	97	98	99	100

7. Describe the pattern in the ones digits.

_____

8. How can you tell whether a number between 1 and 100 is a multiple of 2 without counting up?

_____

9. The multiples of 2 (including zero) are called **even** numbers. Circle the even numbers.

7   3   18   32   21   76   30   89   94   67   15   82

10. The numbers that are not multiples of 2 are called **odd** numbers. Circle the odd numbers.

5   75   60   37   44   68   83   92   100

11. a) Pick two even numbers. Add them. _____ + _____ = _____

b) Is your answer in part a) even or odd? _____

c) If you add two even numbers will you always get an even number? Explain.

_____

_____

12. a) Shade the multiples of 3.

b) What patterns can you see in the positions of the multiples of 3? Use the words "rows," "columns," or "diagonals" in your answer.

_____

_____

_____

_____

_____

1	2	3	4	5	6	7	8	9	10
11	12	13	14	15	16	17	18	19	20
21	22	23	24	25	26	27	28	29	30
31	32	33	34	35	36	37	38	39	40
41	42	43	44	45	46	47	48	49	50
51	52	53	54	55	56	57	58	59	60
61	62	63	64	65	66	67	68	69	70
71	72	73	74	75	76	77	78	79	80
81	82	83	84	85	86	87	88	89	90
91	92	93	94	95	96	97	98	99	100

13. a) Look at the multiples of 3 in the 3rd row of the hundreds chart. Add the tens and ones digits for each of these numbers. What answers do you get?

_$2 + 1 = 3$_____

b) Look at the multiples of 3 in a different row and add the tens and ones digits. If adding gives you a number greater than 10, add the tens and ones digits of that number. What answers did you get? What do you notice?

_____

14. Circle the multiples of 9 in the hundreds chart. What can you say about multiples of 9 and multiples of 3?

_____

15. Add the digits of the multiples of 9 the way you did for the multiples of 3. What do you notice?

_____

16. Fill in the Carroll diagram with the given numbers.

5   75   60   37   45   68   81   92   100

	Multiple of 3	Not a multiple of 3
Multiple of 9		
Not a multiple of 9		

PA4-5 Addition Sequences

Find the **difference** between 15 and 12 by counting on your fingers.

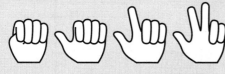

Say: 12   13   14   15

When you say 15, you have 3 fingers up. So the difference or gap between 12 and 15 is 3.

1. Find the difference between the numbers. Write your answer in the circle.

a) 2 ③ 5

b) 3 ⑤ 8

c) 6 ② 8

d) 4 ⑤ 9

e) 12 ④ 16

f) 13 ④ 17

g) 21 ⑤ 26

h) 37 ② 39

i) 26 ③ 29

j) 32 ⑤ 37

k) 24 ⑤ 29

l) 44 ③ 47

m) 51 ④ 55

n) 46 ③ 49

o) 28 ④ 32

p) 34 ⑤ 39 ✓

q) 89 ② 91

r) 62 ⑨ 71

s) 87 ② 89

t) 59 ④ 63

BONUS ▶

u) 96 ⑤ 101

v) 97 ⑤ 102

w) 98 ⑥ 104

x) 117 ⑤ 122

y) 219 ④ 223

z) 146 ⑤ 151

aa) 99 ⑨ 108

bb) 99 ⑧ 107 ✓

2. Why is 17 ◯ 85 harder to solve than 81 ◯ 85?

Because 17 is far away from 85. ✓

What number is 4 **more than** 16? (Or: What is 16 + 4?)

You can find the answer by counting on your fingers. Say 16 with your fist closed, then count up from 16 until you have raised 4 fingers.

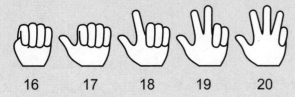

16   17   18   19   20

The number 20 is 4 **more than** 16.

3. Add the number in the circle to the number beside it.

a) 5 ④ _9_

b) 8 ② _10_

c) 7 ③ _10_

d) 3 ④ _7_

e) 17 ⑤ _22_

f) 18 ④ _22_

g) 14 ⑧ _22_

h) 19 ⑥ _25_

i) 30 ⑧ _38_

j) 27 ⑨ _36_

k) 34 ⑦ _4_

l) 32 ⑤ _37_

m) 67 ② _69_

n) 85 ⑤ _90_

o) 42 ③ _45_

p) 68 ④ _27_

q) 54 ⑥ _60_

r) 63 ⑤ _68_

s) 98 ④ _102_

t) 93 ⑧ _101_

BONUS ▶

u) 132 ⑤ _137_

v) 378 ④ _382_

w) 499 ③ _502_

x) 997 ⑤ _1002_

4. Fill in the missing number.

a) _10_ is 4 more than 6

b) _11_ is 6 more than 5

c) _13_ is 5 more than 7

d) _20_ is 1 more than 19

e) _40_ is 6 more than 34

f) _23_ is 5 more than 18

g) _37_ is 8 more than 29

h) _31_ is 7 more than 24

i) _45_ is 8 more than 37

BONUS ▶

j) _____ is 5 more than 168

k) _____ is 9 more than 793

l) _____ is 3 more than 699

m) _____ is 4 more than 9498

In an **increasing sequence**, the next number is always more than the one before. In an **addition sequence**, you add the same number. Continue this addition sequence:

6 , 8 , 10 , 12 , _?_

Step 1: Find the **difference** between the first two numbers.

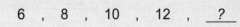

6 , 8 , 10 , 12 , _?_

Step 2: Check that the difference between the other numbers in the pattern is also 2.

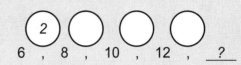

6 , 8 , 10 , 12 , _?_

Step 3: Add 2 to the last number in the sequence.

6 , 8 , 10 , 12 , _14_

5. Extend the pattern. Start by finding the gap between the numbers.

a) 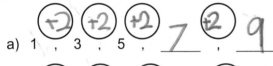 1 , 3 , 5 , 7 , 9

b)  0 , 2 , 4 , 6 , 8

c) 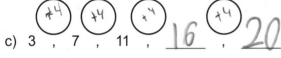 3 , 7 , 11 , 16 , 20

d)  2 , 6 , 10 , 13 , _____

e)  1 , 4 , 7 , 10 , 13

f) 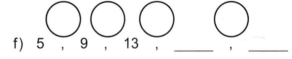 5 , 9 , 13 , _____ , _____

BONUS ▶

g) 1 , 11 , 21 , _____ , _____

h) 5 , 12 , 19 , _____ , _____

i) 21 , 24 , 27 , _____ , _____

j) 86 , 88 , 90 , _____ , _____

6. Dora reads 5 pages of her book each night. Last night she was on page 72.

What page will she reach tonight? Tomorrow night?

_72_	_____	_____
last night	tonight	tomorrow

7. Josh reads 3 pages of his book each night. Last night he was on page 51.

What page will he reach tonight? _____ Tomorrow night? _____

PA4-6 Subtraction Sequences

What number must you subtract from 22 to get 18? 22 − _____ = 18

Evan finds the answer by counting backwards on his fingers.

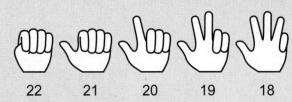

| 22 | 21 | 20 | 19 | 18 |

He could use a number line to help:

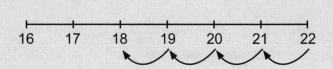

Evan has raised 4 fingers. So 22 − 4 = 18

1. What number must you **subtract** from the greater number to get the lesser number?

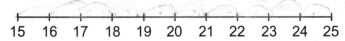

a) 23 ⊖−3 20

b) 24 ⊖-5 19

c) 21 ⊖-5 16

d) 22 ⊖-7 15 ✓

e) 24 ⊖-7 17

f) 19 ⊖-3 16

g) 23 ⊖-6 17

h) 25 ⊖-6 19

2. Find the gap between the numbers.

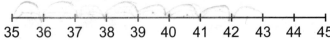

a) 42 ⊖−4 38

b) 41 ⊖-2 39

c) 42 ⊖-5 37

d) 38 ⊖-1 37 ✓

e) 41 ⊖-4 37

f) 40 ⊖-4 36

g) 42 ⊖-7 35

h) 43 ⊖-8 35

3. Find the gap between the numbers.

a) 86 ⊖-5 81

b) 58 ⊖-6 52

c) 50 ⊖-2 48

d) 80 ⊖-2 78

e) 52 ⊖-5 47

f) 67 ⊖-4 63

g) 45 ⊖-9 36

h) 62 ⊖-6 56 ✓

i) 58 ⊖-7 51

j) 101 ⊖-4 97

k) 82 ⊖-6 76

l) 97 ⊖-8 89

Patterns and Algebra 4-6

What number is 3 **less than** 9? (Or: What is 9 − 3?)

Kathy finds the answer by counting on her fingers.

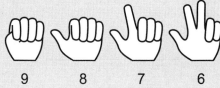

9   8   7   6

The number 6 is 3 **less than** 9.

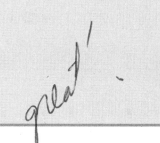
great!

4. Subtract the number in the circle from the number beside it. Write your answer in the blank.

a) 3 ⊙ −2 *2*   b) 12 ⊙ −3 *9*   c) 8 ⊙ −4 *5*   d) 9 ⊙ −1 *8* ✓

e) 8 ⊙ −5 *3*   f) 10 ⊙ −4 ____   g) 5 ⊙ −1 ____   h) 9 ⊙ −2 ____

BONUS ▶

i) 28 ⊙ −4 ____   j) 35 ⊙ −6 ____   k) 57 ⊙ −8 ____   l) 62 ⊙ −4 ____

5. Fill in the missing numbers.

a) _____ is 4 less than 7   b) _____ is 2 less than 9   c) _____ is 5 less than 17

d) _____ is 4 less than 20   e) _____ is 4 less than 32   f) _____ is 5 less than 40

In a **decreasing sequence**, each number is less than the one before it. In a **subtraction sequence**, you subtract the same number.

Let's extend the pattern in this subtraction sequence.   11 , 9 , 7 , _____ , _____

Step 1: Find the gap.   11 ⊙−2 9 ⊙−2 7 ⊙−2 _____ ⊙−2 _____

Step 2: Extend the pattern.   11 ⊙−2 9 ⊙−2 7 ⊙−2 *5* ⊙−2 *3*

---

6. Extend the following subtraction sequences.

a) 10 , 9 , 8 ○ , ____ ○ , ____ ○   b) 14 , 12 , 10 ○ , ____ ○ , ____ ○

c) 23 , 22 , 21 ○ , ____ ○ , ____ ○   d) 24 , 21 , 18 ○ , ____ ○ , ____ ○

Patterns and Algebra 4-6   103

7. Extend the patterns using the gap provided.

Example 1:   6 $\overset{+1}{,}$ 7 , _8_ , _9_

Example 2:   8 $\overset{-2}{,}$ 6 , _4_ , _2_

a) 5 $\overset{+5}{,}$ 10 , _____ , _____ , _____

b) 1 $\overset{+3}{,}$ 4 , _____ , _____ , _____

c) 3 $\overset{+3}{,}$ 6 , _____ , _____ , _____

d) 12 $\overset{-2}{,}$ 10 , _____ , _____ , _____

e) 12 $\overset{+2}{,}$ 14 , _____ , _____ , _____

f) 25 $\overset{-5}{,}$ 20 , _____ , _____ , _____

8. Extend the patterns by first finding the gap.

Example: 3 , 5 , 7 , _____

Step 1:   3 $\overset{+2}{,}$ 5 $\overset{+2}{,}$ 7 , _____

Step 2:   3 , 5 , 7 $\overset{+2}{,}$ _9_

a) 5 , 8 , 11 , _____ , _____

b) 2 , 4 , 6 , _____ , _____

c) 6 , 10 , 14 , _____ , _____

d) 1 , 3 , 5 , _____ , _____

e) 21 , 24 , 27 , _____ , _____

f) 12 , 17 , 22 , _____ , _____

g) 25 , 23 , 21 , _____ , _____

h) 59 , 54 , 49 , _____ , _____

9. Edmond has a box of 24 pears. He eats 3 each day.

How many are left after 5 days? _____

24 , _____ , _____ , _____ , _____ , _____

10. Emma has $17. She saves $4 each day. How much money has she saved after 4 days?

PA4-7 Multiplication Sequences

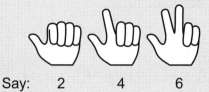

2 × _____ = 6. Find the **multiplier** of 2 to get 6 by skip counting on your fingers.

Say: 2   4   6

When you say 6, you have 3 fingers up. So the multiplier is 3: 2 × 3 = 6.

1. Find the multiplier between the numbers.

a) 2 ⊗×3 6   b) 2 ⊗× 8   c) 5 ⊗× 25   d) 5 ⊗× 40

e) 3 ⊗× 24   f) 3 ⊗× 18   g) 4 ⊗× 28   h) 4 ⊗× 16

i) 6 ⊗× 12   j) 3 ⊗× 9   k) 8 ⊗× 16   l) 3 ⊗× 12

m) 4 ⊗× 20   n) 9 ⊗× 27   o) 3 ⊗× 15   p) 4 ⊗× 24

q) 10 ⊗× 90   r) 10 ⊗× 70   s) 8 ⊗× 80   t) 6 ⊗× 60

u) 1 ⊗× 7   v) 4 ⊗× 24   w) 5 ⊗× 30   x) 8 ⊗× 80

BONUS ▶

y) 6 ⊗× 18   z) 8 ⊗× 32   aa) 9 ⊗× 54   bb) 7 ⊗× 21

2. Multiply the number in the circle by the number beside it. Write your answer in the blank.

a) 5 ⊗×4 _____   b) 8 ⊗×2 _____   c) 7 ⊗×3 _____   d) 3 ⊗×10 _____

e) 4 ⊗×4 _____   f) 9 ⊗×1 _____   g) 6 ⊗×3 _____   h) 6 ⊗×10 _____

i) 3 ⊗×3 _____   j) 6 ⊗×0 _____   k) 2 ⊗×8 _____   l) 5 ⊗×5 _____

m) 1 ⊗×7 _____   n) 7 ⊗×2 _____   o) 4 ⊗×3 _____   p) 5 ⊗×8 _____

3. Extend the pattern. Start by finding the multiplier.

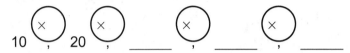

a) 1 ⊗ , 3 ⊗ , 9 ⊗ , _____

b) 1 ⊗ , 2 ⊗ , _____ ⊗ , _____

c) 2 ⊗ , 8 ⊗ , _____

d) 1 ⊗ , 5 ⊗ , _____

e) 2 ⊗ , 6 ⊗ , _____

f) 3 ⊗ , 6 ⊗ , _____

BONUS ▶

10 ⊗ , 20 ⊗ , _____ ⊗ , _____ ⊗ , _____

4. On a TV quiz show, the points double for every question. The 1st question is worth 1 point.

a) What is the 2nd question worth? _____

b) What is the 3rd question worth? _____

c) What is the 5th question worth? _____

5. a) The money that Shelly invests doubles every 10 years. If she starts with $20, how much money will Shelly have after 40 years?

BONUS ▶ How much money will Shelly have if the $20 she invests triples every 10 years?

BONUS ▶ Extend the pattern.

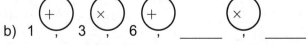

a) 1 ⊗ , 3 ⊕ , 5 ⊗ , _____ ⊕ , _____

b) 1 ⊕ , 3 ⊗ , 6 ⊕ , _____ ⊗ , _____

c) 3 ⊗ , 6 ⊖ , 5 ⊗ , _____ ⊖ , _____

PA4-8 Pattern Rules

1. Continue the sequence by adding the number given.

   a) (add 3)   31, 34, _37_, _4_, _41_   b) (add 5)   70, 75, _80_, _85_, _90_

   c) (add 4)   31, 35, _39_, _43_, _47_   d) (add 9)   11, 20, _29_, _38_, _47_

2. Continue the sequence by subtracting the number given.

   a) (subtract 3)   15, 12, _9_, _6_   b) (subtract 4)   46, 42, _38_, _34_

   c) (subtract 5)   131, 126, _121_, _5_   d) (subtract 7)   49, 42, _35_, _28_

   ~ it seems like you're just subtracting 2 each time.

3. Continue the sequence by multiplying by the number given.

   a) (multiply by 3)   1, 3, _____, _____   b) (multiply by 2)   5, _____, _____

   c) (multiply by 5)   1, _____, _____   d) (multiply by 4)   1, _____, _____

4. Write the first five terms of the pattern, given the pattern rule.

   a) Start at 3. Add 4 each time.   _3_, _____, _____, _____, _____

   b) Start at 27. Subtract 2 each time. _27_, _____, _____, _____, _____

   c) Start at 1. Multiply by 2 each time. _____, _____, _____, _____, _____

   great

BONUS ▶

Make a rule for a pattern. Then make a pattern given by the rule.

My rule: _____

My pattern: _____, _____, _____, _____, _____

5. Which one of the following sequences was made by adding 3? Circle it.
   Hint: Check all the numbers in the sequence.

   A. 3, 5, 9, 12   **B.** 3, 6, 8, 12   **C.** 3, 6, 9, 12

6. What number was added each time to make the pattern?

   a) 2, 5, 8, 11   add _____   b) 15, 17, 19, 21   add _____

   c) 41, 46, 51, 56   add _____   d) 19, 22, 25, 28   add _____

   e) 21, 27, 33, 39   add _____   f) 41, 45, 49, 53   add _____

7. What number was subtracted each time to make the pattern?

    a) 18, 16, 14, 12   subtract _____   b) 35, 30, 25, 20   subtract _____

    c) 100, 99, 98, 97   subtract _____   d) 41, 38, 35, 32   subtract _____

    e) 180, 170, 160, 150   subtract _____   f) 90, 84, 78, 72   subtract _____

8. What number do you multiply by each time to make the pattern?

    a) 1, 5, 25, 125   multiply by _____   b) 2, 6, 18, 54   multiply by _____

    c) 1, 6, 36   multiply by _____   d) 3, 12, 48   multiply by _____

    e) 2, 8, 32   multiply by _____   f) 1, 7, 49   multiply by _____

9. State the rule for the following patterns.

    a) 119, 112, 105, 98, 91 _subtract_ _____   b) 1, 9, 17, 25, 33, 41 _add_ _____

    c) 3, 6, 12, 24 _multiply by_ _____   d) 1, 4, 16, 64 _____

10. Find the rule for the pattern, then fill in the blanks.

    a) 12, 17, 22, _____, _____, _____   The rule is: _Start at 12 and_ _____.

    b) 1, 2, 4, _____, _____, _____   The rule is: _____.

    c) 47, 42, 37, _____, _____, _____   The rule is: _____.

BONUS ▶ In Question 10, which term in part c) will be equal to the first term in part a)?

_____

11. Two sequences start at 5. The first sequence adds 10 each time. The second sequence doubles each time. Which terms in the first sequence are greater than the same terms in the second sequence? Explain.

PA4-9 Introduction to T-tables

Rick makes a growing pattern with blocks.

He records the number of blocks in each figure in a **T-table**.

He writes the number of blocks he adds each time he makes a new figure in a circle.

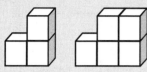 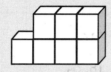

Figure 1   Figure 2   Figure 3

Figure	Number of Blocks
1	3
2	5
3	7

2
2 → number of blocks *added* each time

The number of blocks in the figures are 3, 5, 7, ...

Rick writes a **rule** for this number pattern: *Start at 3 and add 2 each time.*

1. Rick makes another growing pattern with blocks. How many blocks does he add to make each new figure? Write your answer in the circles. Then write a rule for the pattern.

a)

Figure	Number of Blocks
1	3
2	7
3	11

Rule: *Start at 3 and* _____

_____

b)

Figure	Number of Blocks
1	2
2	6
3	10

Rule: _____

_____

c)

Figure	Number of Blocks
1	2
2	4
3	6

Rule: _____

_____

d)

Figure	Number of Blocks
1	1
2	6
3	11

Rule: _____

_____

e)

Figure	Number of Blocks
1	5
2	9
3	13

Rule: _____

_____

f)

Figure	Number of Blocks
1	12
2	18
3	24

Rule: _____

_____

2. Extend the number pattern. How many blocks would be used in the 6ᵗʰ figure?

a)

Figure	Number of Blocks
1	2
2	7
3	12

b)

Figure	Number of Blocks
1	3
2	6
3	9

c)

Figure	Number of Blocks
1	3
2	8
3	13

3. Fill in the missing numbers.

a)

Figure	Number of Blocks
1	2
2	7
3	12
4	
5	22

b)

Figure	Number of Blocks
1	8
2	12
3	
4	
5	24

c)

Figure	Number of Blocks
1	7
2	
3	11
4	
5	15

4. Amy makes an increasing pattern with blocks. After making the 3ʳᵈ figure, she has only 14 blocks left. Does she have enough blocks to complete the 4ᵗʰ figure?

a)

Figure	Number of Blocks
1	3
2	7
3	11

yes   no

b)

Figure	Number of Blocks
1	7
2	10
3	13

yes   no

c)

Figure	Number of Blocks
1	1
2	5
3	9

yes   no

5. How many squares are needed to make the 5ᵗʰ figure in the pattern?
Make a table to show your answer.

a)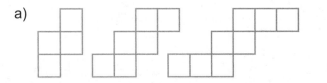

b)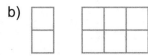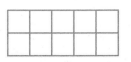

1. Count the number of line segments in each figure. Hint: Count around the outside of the figure first, marking each line segment as you count. Example:

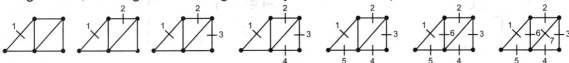

a) 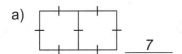 **7**

b) 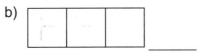 ____

c) 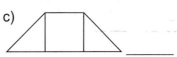 ____

d) 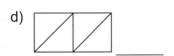 ____

e) 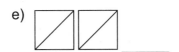 ____

f) 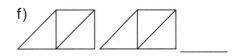 ____

2. Continue the pattern below, then complete the table.

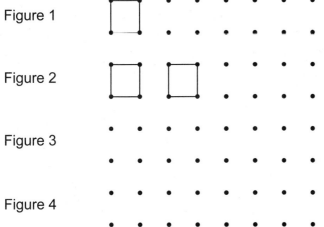

Figure 1

Figure 2

Figure 3

Figure 4

Figure	Number of Line Segments
1	4
2	8
3	
4	

How many line segments would

Figure 5 have? _____

3. Continue the pattern below, then complete the table.

Figure 1

Figure 2

Figure 3

Figure 4

Figure	Number of Line Segments
1	
2	
3	
4	

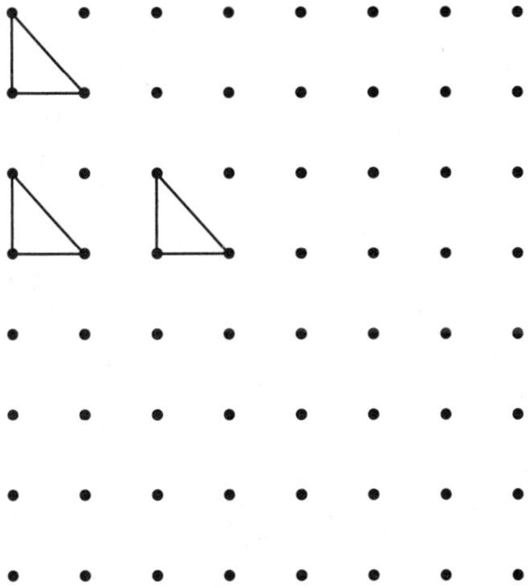

How many line segments would

Figure 5 have? _____

4. Continue the pattern below, then complete the table.

Figure 1

Figure 2

Figure 3

Figure 4

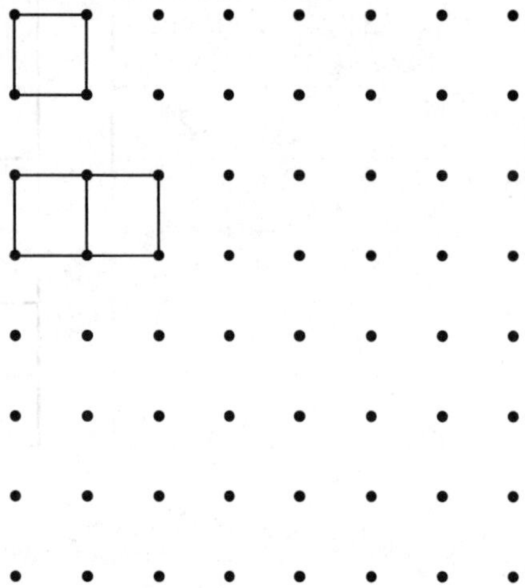

Figure	Number of Line Segments
1	
2	
3	
4	

a) How many line segments would Figure 5 have? _____

b) How many line segments would Figure 6 have? _____

c) How many line segments would Figure 7 have? _____

5. Continue the pattern below, then complete the table.

Figure 1

Figure 2

Figure 3

Figure 4

Figure 5

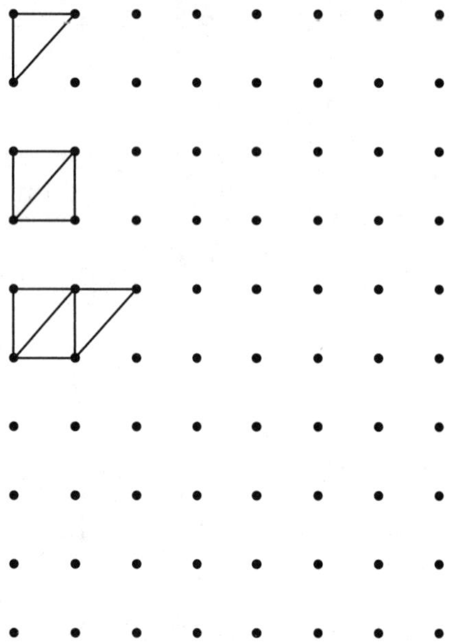

Figure	Number of Line Segments
1	
2	
3	
4	
5	

a) How many line segments would Figure 6 have? _____

b) How many line segments would Figure 7 have? _____

c) How many line segments would Figure 8 have? _____

6. Complete the table. How many young would 5 animals have?

a)

Arctic Fox	Number of Cubs
1	5
2	10

b)

Wood-chuck	Number of Pups
1	4
2	8

c)

White-tailed Deer	Number of Fawns
1	2
2	4

d)

Osprey	Number of Eggs
1	3
2	6

7. Complete the table. How much money would Vicky earn for 4 hours of work?

a)

Hours Worked	Dollars Earned
1	$9

b)

Hours Worked	Dollars Earned
1	$10

c)

Hours Worked	Dollars Earned
1	$8

8. Glen makes a design using triangles and hexagons. He adds two triangles and a hexagon at each stage.

Stage 1:

Stage 2:

Stage 3:

a) Fill in the table.

b) Glen has 6 hexagons and 9 triangles. Does he have enough triangles to use all 6 hexagons? _____

Stage	Hexagons	Triangles
1	1	0
2	2	
3		

9. Hanna makes Christmas ornaments like the one shown. She has 5 trapezoids (the shaded figure). Fill in the table to show how many triangles she will need.

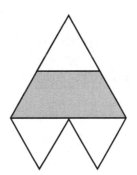

Number of Ornaments	Trapezoids	Triangles

PA4-11 Problem Solving with Patterns

1. A marina rents canoes at $7 for the first hour and $4 for every hour after that. How much would it cost to rent a canoe for 6 hours?

2. A bookstore has a special sale: the first book you buy costs $10 and each book after that costs $5. Arsham has $25.
Does he have enough to buy five books?

3. Draw pictures or make models (using blocks or counters) that match the pattern.

a)

Figure	Number of Objects
1	4
2	6
3	8

b)

Figure	Number of Objects
1	3
2	6
3	9

c)

Figure	Number of Objects
1	4
2	7
3	10

4. Lynn's sapling grows 2 cm in July. It grows 3 cm each month after that. Ray's sapling grows 3 cm in July. It grows 1 cm each month after that. Whose sapling is taller by the end of September?

5. Avril and Jane light a candle the same time. Avril's candle starts at 28 cm tall. It burns down 4 cm every hour. Jane's candle is 21 cm tall when she lights it. It burns down 3 cm every hour. Whose candle is taller after 5 hours?

6. Sandy bikes 20 km on the first day of a trip. She bikes 30 km every day after that. How far has she biked after 4 days?

BONUS ▶ Tristan is 900 km from home on Monday morning. He drives home, travelling 200 km every day.

a) How far from home is he on Wednesday morning?

b) On which day does he arrive home?

Day	Distance from Home in the Morning (km)
Monday	900

Marla knows that 3×6 is 18. Her teacher asks her how she can find 4×6 *quickly* (without adding four 6s).

Marla knows that 4×6 is one more 6 than 3×6. She shows this in two ways:

With a picture:

four 6s { three 6s

plus one more 6

By adding:

$4 \times 6 = 6 + 6 + 6 + 6$

three 6s   plus one more 6

Marla knows that $\mathbf{4 \times 6 = 3 \times 6 + 6}$.

She knows $3 \times 6 = 18$, so $4 \times 6 = 18 + 6 = 24$.

1. Write a product for the array.

a)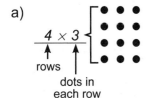

$\dfrac{4 \times 3}{}$
rows   dots in each row

b)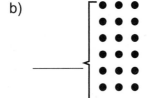

c)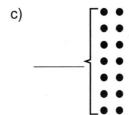

d)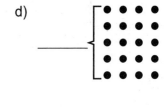

2. Fill in the missing products and number.

a)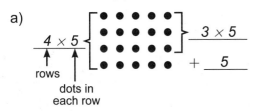

$\dfrac{4 \times 5}{}$
rows   dots in each row

3×5
$+\ \ 5$

b)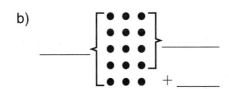

c)

d)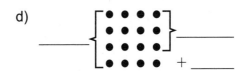

e)

f)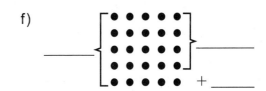

3. Fill in the missing products and number. Then write an equation.

a)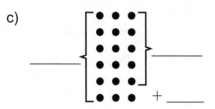

4 × 4   } 3 × 4
        + __4__

_____4 × 4 = (3 × 4) + 4_____

b)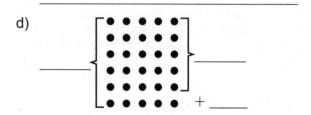

_____ } _____
             + _____

_____

c)

_____ } _____
          + _____

_____

d)

_____ } _____
          + _____

_____

You can always turn a product into a smaller product and a sum.

$$5 × 3 = (\mathbf{4} × 3) + 3$$
take 1 away from 5   add an extra 3

$$9 × 4 = (\mathbf{8} × 4) + 4$$
take 1 away from 9   add an extra 4

---

4. Turn the product into a smaller product and a sum.

a) $4 × 2 = (3 × \underline{\ \ 2\ \ }) + \underline{\ \ 2\ \ }$

b) $5 × 7 = (4 × \underline{\hspace{1.5cm}}) + \underline{\hspace{1.5cm}}$

c) $8 × 3 = (7 × \underline{\hspace{1.5cm}}) + \underline{\hspace{1.5cm}}$

d) $3 × 6 = (2 × \underline{\hspace{1.5cm}}) + \underline{\hspace{1.5cm}}$

e) $7 × 4 = (\underline{\hspace{1cm}} × \underline{\hspace{1cm}}) + \underline{\hspace{1cm}}$

f) $9 × 6 = (\underline{\hspace{1cm}} × \underline{\hspace{1cm}}) + \underline{\hspace{1cm}}$

g) $5 × 5 = \underline{\hspace{4cm}}$

h) $8 × 7 = \underline{\hspace{4cm}}$

i) $7 × 6 = \underline{\hspace{4cm}}$

j) $6 × 4 = \underline{\hspace{4cm}}$

5. Find the answer by turning the product into a smaller product and a sum.

a) $5 × 3 = \underline{\ \ (4 × 3) + 3\ \ }$

   $= \underline{\ \ 12 + 3\ \ }$

   $= \underline{\ \ 15\ \ }$

b) $6 × 3 = \underline{\hspace{3cm}}$

   $= \underline{\hspace{2.5cm}}$

   $= \underline{\hspace{2cm}}$

c) $6 × 4 = \underline{\hspace{3cm}}$

   $= \underline{\hspace{2.5cm}}$

   $= \underline{\hspace{2cm}}$

d) $4 × 4 = \underline{\hspace{3cm}}$

   $= \underline{\hspace{2.5cm}}$

   $= \underline{\hspace{2cm}}$

e) $6 × 6$

f) $3 × 7$

g) $7 × 5$

h) $6 × 8$

REMINDER ▶

$10 \times \square = $ ⟦ ⟧ $10 \times$ ⟦ = □ $10 \times$ □ = ▱

10 × 1 one = 1 ten   10 × 1 ten = 1 hundred   10 × 1 hundred = 1 thousand

1. Draw a model for the multiplication statement, then calculate the answer.

a) $10 \times 30 = 10 \times$ ⟦⟦⟦ = □ □ □ $= \underline{\quad 300 \quad}$

b) $10 \times 200 = 10 \times$ □ □ = ▱ ▱ $= \underline{\qquad}$

c) $10 \times 40 = 10 \times$ ⟦⟦⟦⟦ = $= \underline{\qquad}$

d) $10 \times 5 = 10 \times$ □□□□□ = $= \underline{\qquad}$

e) $10 \times 20 = 10 \times$ ⟦⟦ = $= \underline{\qquad}$

f) $10 \times 4 = 10 \times$ = $= \underline{\qquad}$

2. Multiply.

a) $10 \times 6 = \underline{\qquad}$ b) $10 \times 70 = \underline{\qquad}$ c) $10 \times 800 = \underline{\qquad}$

d) $10 \times 90 = \underline{\qquad}$ e) $10 \times 5 = \underline{\qquad}$ f) $10 \times 400 = \underline{\qquad}$

g) $10 \times 500 = \underline{\qquad}$ **BONUS ▶** $10 \times 20\,000\,000 = \underline{\qquad\qquad\qquad}$

To multiply 3 × 20, David makes 3 groups of 2 tens blocks (20 = 2 tens).

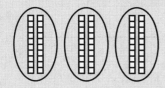

To multiply 3 × 200, David makes 3 groups of 2 hundreds blocks (200 = 2 hundreds).

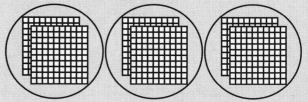

$3 \times 20 = 3 \times 2 \text{ tens} = 6 \text{ tens} = 60$

$3 \times 200 = 3 \times 2 \text{ hundreds} = 6 \text{ hundreds} = 600$

David notices a pattern: $3 \times 2 = 6$ $3 \times 20 = 60$ $3 \times 200 = 600$

3. Draw a model for the multiplication statement, then calculate the answer. The first one is started for you.

a) 4 × 20

b) 2 × 30

$4 \times 20 = 4 \times$ _____ tens = _____ tens = _____

$2 \times 30 = 2 \times$ _____ tens = _____ tens = _____

4. Regroup to find the answer.

a) $3 \times 70 = 3 \times$ __7__ tens = __21__ tens = __210__

b) $3 \times 50 = 3 \times$ _____ tens = _____ tens = _____

c) $5 \times 50 = 5 \times$ _____ tens = _____ tens = _____

d) $4 \times 60 = 4 \times$ _____ tens = _____ tens = _____

5. Complete the pattern by multiplying.

a) $2 \times 2 =$ _____
   $2 \times 20 =$ _____
   $2 \times 200 =$ _____

b) $5 \times 1 =$ _____
   $5 \times 10 =$ _____
   $5 \times 100 =$ _____

c) $2 \times 4 =$ _____
   $2 \times 40 =$ _____
   $2 \times 400 =$ _____

d) $3 \times 3 =$ _____
   $3 \times 30 =$ _____
   $3 \times 300 =$ _____

6. Multiply.

a) $4 \times 30 =$ _____

b) $5 \times 30 =$ _____

c) $4 \times 40 =$ _____

d) $2 \times 50 =$ _____

e) $3 \times 100 =$ _____

f) $4 \times 500 =$ _____

g) $3 \times 60 =$ _____

h) $6 \times 400 =$ _____

i) $2 \times 700 =$ _____

j) $6 \times 70 =$ _____

k) $8 \times 40 =$ _____

l) $2 \times 900 =$ _____

7. Draw a base ten model to show 4 × 200.

8. You know that 3 × 6 = 18. How can you use this fact to multiply 3 × 600?

To multiply 20 × 60, Ren multiplies 2 × (10 × 60).
The picture shows why this works.

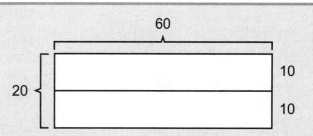

Two 10 × 60 rectangles make one 20 × 60 rectangle.

9. Multiply.

a) $20 \times 60 = 2 \times (10 \times 60)$

   $= 2 \times \underline{\quad 600 \quad}$

   $= \underline{\quad 1200 \quad}$

b) $30 \times 500 = 3 \times (10 \times 500)$

   $= 3 \times \underline{\qquad}$

   $= \underline{\qquad}$

c) $40 \times 800 = 4 \times (10 \times 800)$

   $= 4 \times \underline{\qquad}$

   $= \underline{\qquad}$

d) $30 \times 80 = 3 \times (10 \times 80)$

   $= 3 \times \underline{\qquad}$

   $= \underline{\qquad}$

e) $70 \times 600 = 7 \times (10 \times 600)$

   $= 7 \times \underline{\qquad}$

   $= \underline{\qquad}$

f) $60 \times 700 = 6 \times (10 \times 700)$

   $= 6 \times \underline{\qquad}$

   $= \underline{\qquad}$

To multiply 4 × 700:

Step 1: Multiply 4 × 7 = 28.
Step 2: Write all the zeros from 4 and 700 in the answer: 4 × **700** = 28**00**.

10. Multiply the 1-digit numbers to multiply the larger numbers.

a) $8 \times 5 = \underline{\quad 40 \quad}$

   $800 \times 5 = \underline{\quad 4000 \quad}$

b) $2 \times 3 = \underline{\qquad}$

   $2 \times 300 = \underline{\qquad}$

c) $5 \times 2 = \underline{\qquad}$

   $5 \times 200 = \underline{\qquad}$

d) $8 \times 7 = \underline{\qquad}$

   $800 \times 7 = \underline{\qquad}$

e) $4 \times 9 = \underline{\qquad}$

   $4 \times 900 = \underline{\qquad}$

f) $5 \times 6 = \underline{\qquad}$

   $50 \times 600 = \underline{\qquad}$

g) $40 \times 30 = \underline{\qquad}$

h) $300 \times 50 = \underline{\qquad}$

i) $80 \times 500 = \underline{\qquad}$

j) $800 \times 900 = \underline{\qquad}$

k) $50 \times 5000 = \underline{\qquad}$

l) $40 \times 50\ 000 = \underline{\qquad}$

BONUS ▶ $3000 \times 80\ 000 = \underline{\qquad\qquad\qquad}$

11. Multiply.

a) 3142×1000

   $= \underline{\qquad\qquad}$

b) 2984×1000

   $= \underline{\qquad\qquad}$

c) $70\ 162 \times 1000$

   $= \underline{\qquad\qquad}$

1. Write a product for the array.

a)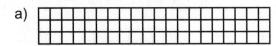

  3 × 20

b)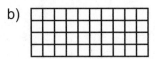

  _____

c)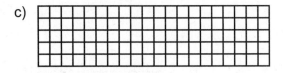

  _____

d)

  _____

2. Write a product for the whole array and for each part of the array.

a) 3 × 24

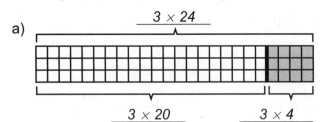

  3 × 20   3 × 4

b) _____

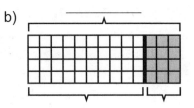

  _____   _____

c) _____

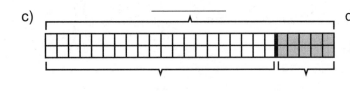

  _____   _____

d) _____

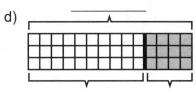

  _____   _____

3. Fill in the blanks.

a) 2 × 24

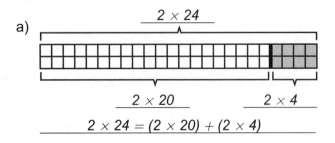

  2 × 20   2 × 4

  2 × 24 = (2 × 20) + (2 × 4)

b) _____

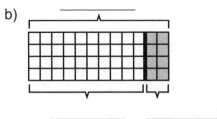

  _____   _____

  _____

c) 4 × 25

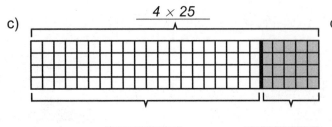

  _____   _____

  _____

d) _____

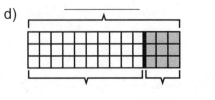

  _____   _____

  _____

To multiply 3×23, Shelly rewrites 23 as a sum:

$23 = 20 + 3$

She multiplies 20 by 3, and then she multiplies 3 by 3:

$3 \times 20 = 60$ and $3 \times 3 = 9$

Finally, she adds the results: $60 + 9 = 69$

The picture shows why Shelly's method works:

$3 \times 23 = (3 \times 20) + (3 \times 3) = 60 + 9 = 69$

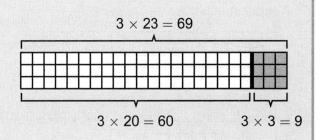

$3 \times 23 = 69$

$3 \times 20 = 60$ $3 \times 3 = 9$

4. Rewrite the multiplication statement as a sum.

a) $2 \times 24 = \underline{\quad 2 \times 20 \quad} + \underline{\quad 2 \times 4 \quad}$ b) $2 \times 23 = \underline{\qquad\qquad} + \underline{\qquad\qquad}$

c) $3 \times 32 = \underline{\qquad\qquad} + \underline{\qquad\qquad}$ d) $4 \times 12 = \underline{\qquad\qquad} + \underline{\qquad\qquad}$

5. Multiply using Shelly's method.

a) $3 \times 13 = \underline{\quad 3 \times 10 \quad} + \underline{\quad 3 \times 3 \quad} = \underline{\quad 30 + 9 \quad} = \underline{\qquad 39 \qquad}$

b) $3 \times 21 = \underline{\qquad\qquad} + \underline{\qquad\qquad} = \underline{\qquad\qquad} = \underline{\qquad\qquad\qquad}$

c) $2 \times 14 = \underline{\qquad\qquad} + \underline{\qquad\qquad} = \underline{\qquad\qquad} = \underline{\qquad\qquad\qquad}$

d) $3 \times 213 = \underline{\quad 3 \times 200 \quad} + \underline{\quad 3 \times 10 \quad} + \underline{\quad 3 \times 3 \quad} = \underline{\quad 600 + 30 + 9 \quad} = \underline{\quad 639 \quad}$

e) $2 \times 231 = \underline{\qquad\qquad} + \underline{\qquad\qquad} + \underline{\qquad\qquad} = \underline{\qquad\qquad\qquad} = \underline{\qquad\qquad}$

f) $2 \times 342 = \underline{\qquad\qquad} + \underline{\qquad\qquad} + \underline{\qquad\qquad} = \underline{\qquad\qquad\qquad} = \underline{\qquad\qquad}$

6. Multiply in your head by multiplying the digits separately.

a) $3 \times 12 = \underline{\qquad}$ b) $2 \times 31 = \underline{\qquad}$ c) $4 \times 12 = \underline{\qquad}$ d) $5 \times 11 = \underline{\qquad}$

e) $4 \times 21 = \underline{\qquad}$ f) $2 \times 43 = \underline{\qquad}$ g) $2 \times 32 = \underline{\qquad}$ h) $3 \times 33 = \underline{\qquad}$

i) $4 \times 112 = \underline{\qquad}$ j) $2 \times 234 = \underline{\qquad}$ k) $3 \times 233 = \underline{\qquad}$ l) $5 \times 111 = \underline{\qquad}$

m) $3 \times 132 = \underline{\qquad}$ n) $2 \times 422 = \underline{\qquad}$ o) $4 \times 212 = \underline{\qquad}$ p) $3 \times 333 = \underline{\qquad}$

7. Lela planted 223 trees in each of 3 rows. How many trees did she plant altogether?

8. Josh put 240 marbles in each of 2 bags. How many marbles did he put in the bags?

1. Double the number.

   a) double 3 is _____   b) double 2 is _____   c) double 6 is _____

   d) double 4 is _____   e) double 7 is _____   f) double 8 is _____

2. Double the number mentally by doubling the ones digit and the tens digit separately.

   a) double 24 is _____   b) double 14 is _____   c) double 12 is _____

   d) double 13 is _____   e) double 51 is _____   f) double 43 is _____

   g) double 71 is _____   h) double 84 is _____   i) double 93 is _____

3. Double the ones and tens separately and add the result.

   a) double 16 is _20 + 12 = 32_ b) double 26 is _____   c) double 37 is _____

   d) double 29 is _____   e) double 48 is _____   f) double 19 is _____

   g) double 57 is _____   h) double 67 is _____   i) double 89 is _____

If you know 3 times a number, you can double to find 6 times the number.

$3 \times 7 = 21$
so $6 \times 7 = 42$

---

4. Double 3 times the number to find 6 times the number.

   a) $3 \times 2 =$ _____   b) $3 \times 5 =$ _____   c) $3 \times 9 =$ _____

   so $6 \times 2 =$ _____   so $6 \times 5 =$ _____   so $6 \times 9 =$ _____

   d) $3 \times 4 =$ _____   e) $3 \times 6 =$ _____   f) $3 \times 8 =$ _____

   so $6 \times 4 =$ _____   so $6 \times 6 =$ _____   so $6 \times 8 =$ _____

5. Double 2 times the number to find 4 times the number. Then find 8 times the number by doubling again.

   a) $2 \times 7 =$ _____   b) $2 \times 8 =$ _____   c) $2 \times 6 =$ _____

   so $4 \times 7 =$ _____   so $4 \times 8 =$ _____   so $4 \times 6 =$ _____

   and $8 \times 7 =$ _____   and $8 \times 8 =$ _____   and $8 \times 6 =$ _____

d) $2 \times 11 =$ _____

   so $4 \times 11 =$ _____

   and $8 \times 11 =$ _____

e) $2 \times 9 =$ _____

   so $4 \times 9 =$ _____

   and $8 \times 9 =$ _____

f) $2 \times 12 =$ _____

   so $4 \times 12 =$ _____

   and $8 \times 12 =$ _____

6. Double 3 times the number to find 6 times the number. Then find 12 times the number.

a) $3 \times 7 =$ _____

   so $6 \times 7 =$ _____

   and $12 \times 7 =$ _____

b) $3 \times 8 =$ _____

   so $6 \times 8 =$ _____

   and $12 \times 8 =$ _____

c) $3 \times 11 =$ _____

   so $6 \times 11 =$ _____

   and $12 \times 11 =$ _____

d) $3 \times 6 =$ _____

   so $6 \times 6 =$ _____

   and $12 \times 6 =$ _____

e) $3 \times 9 =$ _____

   so $6 \times 9 =$ _____

   and $12 \times 9 =$ _____

f) $3 \times 12 =$ _____

   so $6 \times 12 =$ _____

   and $12 \times 12 =$ _____

7. Use doubling to find 16 times the number.

a) 3

   $2 \times 3 = 6$

   $4 \times 3 = 12$

   $8 \times 3 = 24$

   $16 \times 3 = 48$

b) 7

c) 9

d) 13

e) 17

f) 19

8. Use doubling to calculate the total cost mentally.

a) 2 candies for 42¢ each

b) 2 pencils for 37¢ each

c)

   48¢   ?

d) 8 stickers for 7¢ each

e) 12 candies for 9¢ each

BONUS ▶ Use doubling to find 128×13.

The Standard Method for Multiplication (No Regrouping)

Clara uses a chart to multiply 3 × 42:

Step 1: She multiplies the ones digit of 42 by 3. (3 × 2 = 6)

Step 2: She multiplies the tens digit of 42 by 3. (3 × 4 tens = 12 tens)

She regroups 10 tens as 1 hundred.

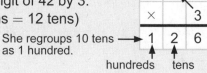

hundreds   tens

1. Use Clara's method to find the product.

a)   3 1
   ×   4

b)   5 3
   ×   2

c)   4 1
   ×   4

d)   2 1
   ×   6

e)   3 1
   ×   3

f)   7 1
   ×   2

g)   6 2
   ×   3

h)   8 4
   ×   2

i)   5 2
   ×   4

j)   2 2
   ×   2

k)   2 1
   ×   5

l)   5 3
   ×   3

m)   4 2
   ×   4

n)   4 3
   ×   3

o)   6 4
   ×   2

p)   7 3
   ×   3

q)   5 4
   ×   2

r)   6 2
   ×   4

s)   7 2
   ×   3

t)   9 1
   ×   2

u)   6 3
   ×   3

v)   8 1
   ×   2

w)   5 1
   ×   5

x)   7 2
   ×   4

y)   6 1
   ×   5

z)   7 2
   ×   2

aa)   8 3
   ×   3

bb)   9 1
   ×   9

cc)   4 1
   ×   6

dd)   6 1
   ×   8

ee)   9 2
   ×   4

ff)   8 5
   ×   1

gg)   4 3
   ×   2

hh)   6 1
   ×   7

ii)   7 1
   ×   8

2. Find the product.

a) 2 × 62   b) 2 × 74   c) 4 × 21   d) 4 × 62   e) 5 × 41   f) 7 × 21

NS4-26 Multiplication with Regrouping

Fred uses a chart to multiply 3 × 24:

Step 1: He multiplies 4 ones by 3. (4 × 3 = 12)

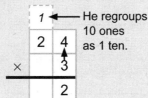

He regroups 10 ones as 1 ten.

Step 2: He multiplies 2 tens by 3. (3 × 2 tens = 6 tens)

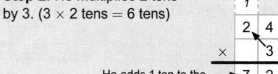

He adds 1 ten to the result. (6 + 1 = 7 tens)

---

1. Using Fred's method, complete the first step of the multiplication.

a)
```
    2
  1 4
×   5
─────
    0
```

b)
```
  1 4
×   3
─────
```

c)
```
  1 5
×   3
─────
```

d)
```
  3 6
×   2
─────
```

e)
```
  2 5
×   4
─────
```

2. Using Fred's method, complete the second step of the multiplication.

a)
```
    1
  2 4
×   4
─────
    6
```

b)
```
    1
  1 2
×   5
─────
    0
```

c)
```
    2
  1 4
×   5
─────
    0
```

d)
```
    2
  1 4
×   6
─────
    4
```

e)
```
    1
  2 5
×   3
─────
    5
```

f)
```
    1
  3 5
×   2
─────
    0
```

g)
```
    1
  4 7
×   2
─────
    4
```

h)
```
    2
  1 8
×   3
─────
    4
```

i)
```
    2
  2 7
×   3
─────
    1
```

j)
```
    3
  1 6
×   5
─────
    0
```

3. Using Fred's method, complete the first and second steps of the multiplication.

a)
```
  2 5
×   2
─────
```

b)
```
  1 6
×   6
─────
```

c)
```
  3 5
×   4
─────
```

d)
```
  3 5
×   3
─────
```

e)
```
  4 2
×   3
─────
```

f)
```
  3 4
×   3
─────
```

g)
```
  3 2
×   5
─────
```

h)
```
  3 7
×   6
─────
```

i)
```
  8 2
×   5
─────
```

j)
```
  2 3
×   7
─────
```

Multiplying with the 6, 7, 8, and 9 Times Tables

1. Finish the 3 times table. Double the 3 times table to write the 6 times table.

	1	2	3	4	5	6	7	8	9
the number × 3	3	6	9						
the number × 6	6	12	18						

2. Multiply by 6.

a)
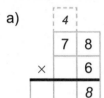

b)

c)
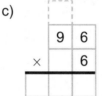

d)
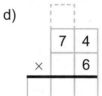

e)
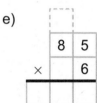

f)
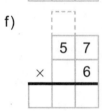

g)
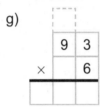

h)
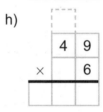

i)
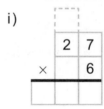

j)
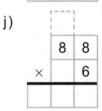

3. Cover the top of this page and multiply. Use grid paper to line up the place values.

a) 37 × 6   b) 98 × 6   c) 79 × 6   d) 85 × 6   e) 46 × 6

4. Finish the 2 times table. Double the 2 times table to write the 4 times table.
Then double again to write the 8 times table.

	1	2	3	4	5	6	7	8	9
the number × 2	2	4	6						
the number × 4	4	8	12						
the number × 8	8	16	24						

5. Multiply by 8.

a)
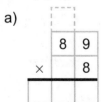

b)
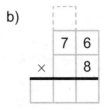

c)

d)

e)

6. Multiply by 8. Only look at the times table when you need to. Use grid paper to line up the place values.

a) 99×8 b) 69×8 c) 68×8 d) 87×8 e) 77×8

7. Continue the pattern in the tens digits and the ones digits to write the 9 times table.

$1 \times 9 =$ _____ ___9___ $6 \times 9 =$ _____ _____

$2 \times 9 =$ ___1___ ___8___ $7 \times 9 =$ _____ _____

$3 \times 9 =$ ___2___ ___7___ $8 \times 9 =$ _____ _____

$4 \times 9 =$ _____ _____ $9 \times 9 =$ _____ _____

$5 \times 9 =$ _____ _____ $10 \times 9 =$ _____ _____

8. Multiply by 9.

a)

```
    7 9
  ×   9
  ─────
```

b)

```
    6 8
  ×   9
  ─────
```

c)

d)

e)

f)

```
    8 8
  ×   9
  ─────
```

g)

```
    6 6
  ×   9
  ─────
```

h)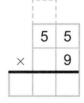

i)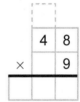

j)

REMINDER ▶ If you know 7×9, then you know 9×7 too.

---

9. Use $7 \times 7 = 49$ and all the other times tables to write the 7 times table.

	1	2	3	4	5	6	7	8	9
the number $\times$ 7									

10. Use grid paper to multiply by 7. Only use the times table when you need to.

a) 36×7 b) 48×7 c) 27×7 d) 81×7 e) 18×7

f) 85×7 g) 76×7 h) 59×7 i) 94×7 j) 39×7

Kim multiplies 2×213 in three different ways.

1. With a chart:

hundreds	tens	ones
2	1	3
×		2
4	2	6

2. In expanded form:

$$200 + 10 + 3$$
$$\times\ 2$$
$$= 400 + 20 + 6$$
$$= 426$$

3. With base ten blocks:

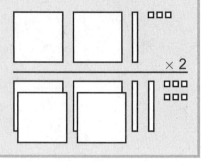

1. Rewrite the multiplication in expanded form. Then multiply.

   a) 321   _____ + _____ + _____   b) 432   _____ + _____ + _____
      × 3   _____ × 3   × 2   _____ × 2

                  = _____ + _____ + _____   = _____ + _____ + _____
                  = _____   = _____

2. Draw a picture to show the result of the multiplication.

   a) 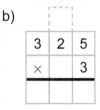 × 3

   b) 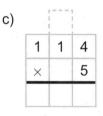 × 3

   c) 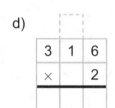 × 3

3. Multiply.

   a)
1	2	4
×		2

   b)
2	1	3
×		3

   c)
1	2	2
×		4

   d)
3	2	3
×		3

   e)
4	1	3
×		2

4. Multiply. Regroup ones as tens.

   a)
	1	
1	2	3
×		4
4	9	2

   b)
3	2	5
×		3

   c)
1	1	4
×		5

   d)
3	1	6
×		2

   e)
1	1	5
×		6

5. Multiply. Regroup tens as hundreds.

   a)
2	4	1
×		4

   b)
1	5	1
×		5

   c)
2	4	2
×		3

   d)
1	5	2
×		3

   e)
2	5	3
×		3

6. Copy the question onto grid paper. Multiply, regrouping where you need to.

a) 347 × 2   b) 263 × 3   c) 117 × 5   d) 232 × 4   e) 172 × 4   f) 317 × 3

Sometimes, you need to regroup hundreds as thousands. When there are no other thousands, you don't need to show the regrouping on top—you can put the regrouping in the answer right away.

Example:
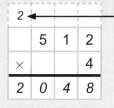
— You don't need to write this 2 here, because there are no other thousands to add to it.

7. a) Circle the products you expect to be greater than 1000.

i) 841 × 2   ii) 283 × 3   iii) 731 × 5   iv) 916 × 4   v) 237 × 4

b) Multiply. Regroup where you need to.

i)    ii)    iii) 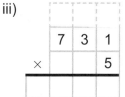   iv) 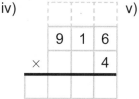   v)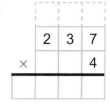

 c) Were your predictions in part a) correct? If not, was the mistake in your calculation or your estimation strategy?

Sometimes you need to regroup two or three times.

Example 1: 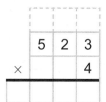   Example 2:

8. Multiply. You will need to copy parts f) to j) onto grid paper.

a)    b)   c)   d)   e)

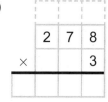

 f) 4 × 247   g) 5 × 841   h) 7 × 213   i) 8 × 134   j) 3 × 738

9. Complete the 6, 7, 8, and 9 times tables.

	1	2	3	4	5	6	7	8	9
the number × 6									
the number × 7									
the number × 8									
the number × 9									

10. Multiply. Regroup where you need to.

a)
```
    8  1  3
 ×        6
 ──────────
```

b)
```
    8  0  9
 ×        7
 ──────────
```

c)
```
    6  8  7
 ×        8
 ──────────
```

d)
```
    8  7  9
 ×        8
 ──────────
```

e)
```
    6  1  5
 ×        6
 ──────────
```

f)
```
    7  1  3
 ×        7
 ──────────
```

g)
```
    6  8  7
 ×        9
 ──────────
```

BONUS ▶
```
    2  6  1  7
 ×           8
 ─────────────
```

11. An octopus has 8 arms and 240 suckers on each arm.
How many suckers does an octopus have?

12. Lynn can read 937 words in an hour.
How many words can she read in 8 hours?

13. A factory produces 847 ice cream bars in a day.
How many ice cream bars does the factory produce in 6 days?

14. Marcel collected 842 shirts for charity. Each shirt has 7 buttons.
How many buttons were there?

1. Estimate by rounding the larger number to the nearest 10.

a) 52 → [50]
    × 3   × 3
          [150]

b) 67 → [ ]
    × 5   × 5
          [ ]

c) 93 → [ ]
    × 6   × 6
          [ ]

d) 29 → [ ]
    × 8   × 8
          [ ]

e) 32 × 5
    ≈ __30 × 5__
    = _____

f) 74 × 3
    ≈ _____
    = _____

g) 37 × 4
    ≈ _____
    = _____

h) 84 × 6
    ≈ _____
    = _____

i) 19 × 9
    ≈ _____
    = _____

j) 38 × 7
    ≈ _____
    = _____

k) 8 × 56
    ≈ _____
    = _____

l) 5 × 85
    ≈ _____
    = _____

BONUS ▶

m) 234 × 4
    ≈ __230 × 4__
    = _____

n) 366 × 7
    ≈ _____
    = _____

o) 195 × 8
    ≈ _____
    = _____

p) 6 × 473
    ≈ _____
    = _____

2. Estimate by rounding the 3-digit number to the nearest 100.

a) 152 → [200]
    × 3   × 3
           [600]

b) 367 → [ ]
    × 5   × 5
           [ ]

c) 493 → [ ]
    × 6   × 6
           [ ]

d) 729 → [ ]
    × 8   × 8
           [ ]

e) 732 × 5
    ≈ __700 × 5__
    = __3500__

f) 174 × 3
    ≈ _____
    = _____

g) 837 × 4
    ≈ _____
    = _____

h) 584 × 6
    ≈ _____
    = _____

i) 419 × 9
    ≈ _____
    = _____

j) 138 × 7
    ≈ _____
    = _____

k) 8 × 956
    ≈ _____
    = _____

l) 5 × 785
    ≈ _____
    = _____

3. Round the 2-digit number up and down to find high and low estimates for the product.

a) $\underline{\quad 50 \quad} < \quad 57 \quad < \underline{\quad 60 \quad}$

so $\underline{\quad 50 \quad} \times 3 < 57 \times 3 < \underline{\quad 60 \quad} \times 3$

$\underline{\quad 150 \quad} < 57 \times 3 < \underline{\quad 180 \quad}$

b) $\underline{\qquad} < \quad 63 \quad < \underline{\qquad}$

so $\underline{\qquad} \times 7 < 63 \times 7 < \underline{\qquad} \times 7$

$\underline{\qquad} < 63 \times 7 < \underline{\qquad}$

c) $\underline{\qquad} < \quad 39 \quad < \underline{\qquad}$

so $\underline{\qquad} \times 9 < 39 \times 9 < \underline{\qquad} \times 9$

$\underline{\qquad} < 39 \times 9 < \underline{\qquad}$

d) $\underline{\qquad} < \quad 21 \quad < \underline{\qquad}$

so $\underline{\qquad} \times 8 < 21 \times 8 < \underline{\qquad} \times 8$

$\underline{\qquad} < 21 \times 8 < \underline{\qquad}$

e) $\underline{\qquad} \times 5 < 48 \times 5 < \underline{\qquad} \times 5$

$\underline{\qquad} < 48 \times 5 < \underline{\qquad}$

f) $\underline{\qquad} \times 6 < 75 \times 6 < \underline{\qquad} \times 6$

$\underline{\qquad} < 75 \times 6 < \underline{\qquad}$

4. Grace donated 78 books to charity. If each book is then sold for $4, approximately how much money did the charity make?

5. Sam bought 4 pair of jeans for $89 each. Approximately how much did he spend?

6. A store sells cooked hot dogs for $3 each. You can buy a package of 12 uncooked hot dogs for $18. Estimate the cost of 12 cooked hot dogs. Which is cheaper? Can you be sure without calculating the actual cost?

7. Nina multiplies the following numbers:

   i) $27 \times 6 = 302$ ii) $73 \times 8 = 584$ iii) $81 \times 9 = 727$ iv) $67 \times 4 = 268$

   a) Use estimation to decide if her answers are reasonable.

   b) Multiply to see if her answers are correct.

   BONUS ▶ Can an answer be reasonable but still incorrect? Explain.

8. Lewis reads around 7 pages a day.

   a) Estimate how many pages he will read in February.

   b) Estimate how many pages he will read in July.

   c) February is the shortest month of the year. July is the longest month of the year. Approximately how many pages will Lewis read in a regular month?

   d) There are 12 months in the year. Estimate how many pages Lewis will read in a year.

   e) There are 365 days in a year. Use this number to estimate how many pages Lewis will read in a year.

NS4-30 Word Problems with Multiplying

1. Raj bikes 372 metres each day. How many metres does he bike in four days?

2. On average, every Canadian uses 251 litres of water each day.

  a) About how much water does each Canadian use in a week?

  b) About how much water would a family of 4 use in a day?

3. a) The product of 3 and 2 is 6 because $3 \times 2 = 6$. The sum of 3 and 2 is 5 because $3 + 2 = 5$. Which is greater: the sum or the product?

  b) Try finding the sum and the product of different pairs of numbers. (For example, try 3 and 4, 2 and 5, 5 and 6, 1 and 7.) What do you notice? Is the product always greater than the sum?

4. Ella multiplied two numbers, both not zero. The product was one of the numbers. What was the other number?

5. Write all the pairs of numbers you can think of that multiply to give 20.
BONUS ▶ Find all pairs of numbers that multiply to give 40.

6. A cicada can burrow into the ground and stay there for 10 years.

  a) How many months can a cicada stay in the ground?

  b) Sometimes, cicadas stay in the ground for up to 20 years. How can you use your answer in part a) to find out how many months this is?

7. There are 4 ways to put 6 dots into arrays so that each row contains the same number of dots.

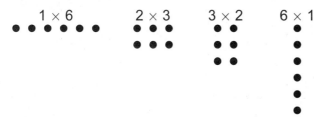

1×6 2×3 3×2 6×1

How many ways can you put the dots into one or more equal rows?
Write a multiplication statement for each array.

  a) 4 dots   b) 8 dots   c) 12 dots   d) 16 dots

8. Rob rode a horse around a six-sided field with each side 355 metres long. How far did he ride?

9. Kyle has 2 stickers. Rani has 8 stickers.

Rani has _____ times as many stickers as Kyle.

10. A bee has 6 legs. How many legs do 32 bees have?

11. A harp has 47 strings. How many strings do 8 harps have?

12. Explain why the product of two 2-digit numbers must be at least 100.

_____

_____

13. A hummingbird flaps its wings 15 times a second. How many times does it flap its wings in a minute?

14. How many hours are there in the month of January?

15. Use the digits 3, 4, and 5 to make …

   a) the greatest product

   ⬚ × ⬚⬚

   b) the least product

   ⬚ × ⬚⬚

16. Use the digits 1, 2, 3, and 4 to make …

   a) the greatest product

   ⬚ × ⬚⬚⬚

   b) the least product

   ⬚ × ⬚⬚⬚

17. Find the first three products. Use the pattern in the products to find the products in parts d), e), and f) without multiplying.

a)
```
    3 7
  ×   3
```

b)
```
    3 7
  ×   6
```

c)
```
    3 7
  ×   9
```

d)
```
    3 7
  × 1 2
```

e)
```
    3 7
  × 1 5
```

f)
```
    3 7
  × 1 8
```

18. Find the product.

   a) $0 \times 5 =$ _____

   b) $0 \times 7 =$ _____

   c) $0 \times 9 =$ _____

   d) $17 \times 0 =$ _____

19. Jasmin multiplied a number by 5 and got 0. What was the original number? _____

NS4-31 Sets and Sharing

Ella has 12 glasses of water. A tray holds 3 glasses. There are 4 trays.

Question:

What has been shared or divided into **sets** or **groups**?
How many sets are there?
How many things are in each set?

Answer:

Glasses
There are 4 sets of glasses.
There are 3 glasses in each set.

1. a)

What has been shared into sets?

_____

How many sets? _____

How many in each set? _____

b)

What has been divided into sets?

_____

How many sets? _____

How many in each set? _____

2. Using circles for sets or groups and dots for things, draw a picture to show …

a) 4 sets
6 things in each set

b) 6 groups
3 things in each group

c) 6 sets
2 things in each set

d) 4 groups
5 things in each group

3. Complete the table.

		What has been divided into sets?	How many sets?	How many in each set?
a)	20 toys 4 toys for each child 5 children	*20 toys*	*5*	*4*
b)	7 friends 21 pencils 3 pencils for each friend			
c)	16 students 4 desks 4 students at each desk			
d)	8 plants 24 flowers 3 flowers on each plant			
e)	6 grapefruits in each box 42 grapefruits 7 boxes			
f)	3 school buses 30 children 10 children in each school bus			
g)	6 puppies in each litter 6 litters 36 puppies			
h)	28 markers 4 kids 7 markers for each kid			
i)	4 boxes 24 markers 6 markers in each box			

BONUS ▶ Draw pictures for Question 3 parts a), b), and c) using circles for sets and dots for the things being divided.

Kate wants to share 12 cookies with 3 friends.
She sets out 4 plates (one for herself and one for each of her friends).

She puts 1 cookie at
a time on each plate:

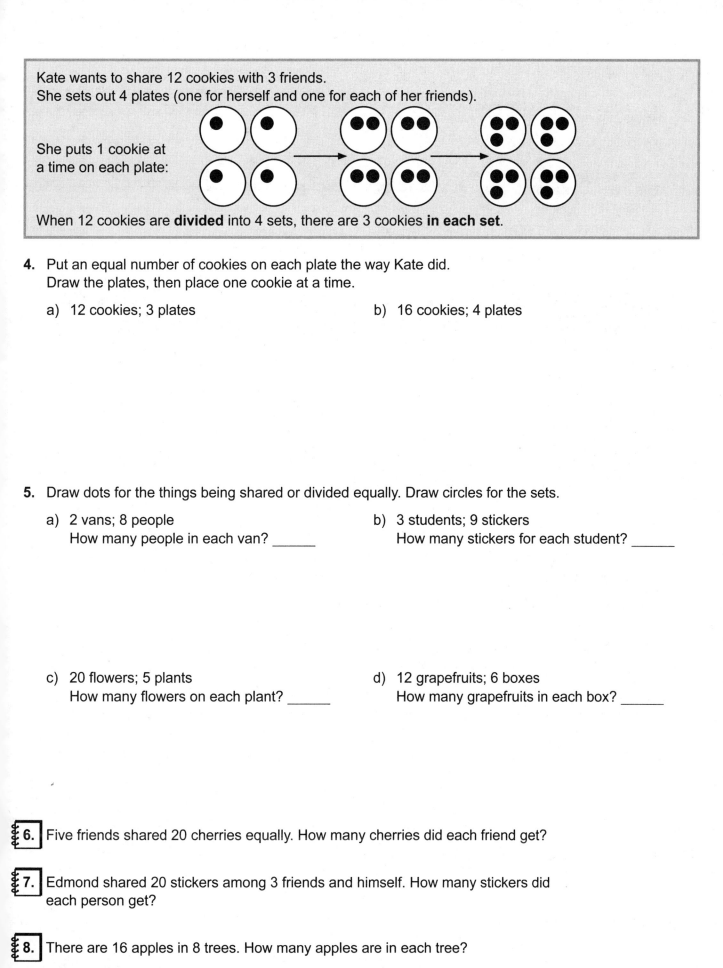

When 12 cookies are **divided** into 4 sets, there are 3 cookies **in each set**.

4. Put an equal number of cookies on each plate the way Kate did.
   Draw the plates, then place one cookie at a time.

   a) 12 cookies; 3 plates

   b) 16 cookies; 4 plates

5. Draw dots for the things being shared or divided equally. Draw circles for the sets.

   a) 2 vans; 8 people
      How many people in each van? _____

   b) 3 students; 9 stickers
      How many stickers for each student? _____

   c) 20 flowers; 5 plants
      How many flowers on each plant? _____

   d) 12 grapefruits; 6 boxes
      How many grapefruits in each box? _____

6. Five friends shared 20 cherries equally. How many cherries did each friend get?

7. Edmond shared 20 stickers among 3 friends and himself. How many stickers did
   each person get?

8. There are 16 apples in 8 trees. How many apples are in each tree?

Sam has 30 apples. He wants to give 5 apples to each of his friends.

To find out how many friends he can give apples to, he takes away **sets** (or **groups**) of 5 apples until he has no apples left.

He can give apples to 6 friends. When 30 apples are divided into sets of 5 apples, there are 6 sets.

9. Put the correct number of dots in each set.

a)   b) ● ● ● ● ● ● ● ● ● ●   c) ● ● ● ● ● ● ● ● ● ● ● ●

    4 dots in each set   5 dots in each set   3 dots in each set

10. Draw circles to divide these arrays into …

   a) groups of 3   b) groups of 4   c) groups of 3   d) groups of 4

11. Draw dots for the things being shared or divided equally. Draw circles for the sets.

   a) 15 apples; 5 apples in each box   b) 10 stickers; 2 stickers for each student
      How many boxes?   How many students?

     _____ boxes   _____ students

12. Shelly has 18 cookies. She gives 3 cookies to each of her siblings.
How many siblings does she have?

13. Matt has 14 stamps. He puts 2 stamps on each envelope.
How many envelopes does he have?

NS4-32 Two Ways to Share

Tristan has 15 cookies. There are two ways he can share or **divide** the cookies equally:

Method 1: Decide how many sets (or groups) **to make.**

Example: Tristan wants to make 3 sets of cookies. He draws 3 circles: He puts one cookie at a time into the circles until he has placed all 15 cookies.

Method 2: Decide how many will be in each set.

Example: Tristan wants to put 5 cookies in each set. He counts out 5 cookies: He counts out sets of 5 until he has placed all 15 cookies.

Use Method 1 to do Questions 1, 2, and 3.

1. Share **20** dots equally. How many dots are in each set? Hint: Place one dot at a time.

   a) 4 sets:

   There are _____ dots in each set.

   b) 5 sets:

   There are _____ dots in each set.

2. Divide the triangles equally among the sets. Hint: Count the triangles first.

   a)

   b)

3. Divide the squares equally among the sets.

Use Method 2 to do Questions 4 and 5.

4. Group the lines so that there are 3 lines in each set.

   a) | | | | | | | | |

   There are _____ sets.

   b) | | | | | | | | | | | |

   There are _____ sets.

   c) | | | | | |

   There are _____ sets.

5. Group **12** dots so that …

   a) there are 6 dots in each set.

   b) there are 4 dots in each set.

6. For each part, fill in what you know. Write a question mark for what you don't know.

		What has been shared or divided into sets?	How many sets?	How many in each set?
a)	Vicky has 25 pencils. She puts 5 pencils in each box.	25 pencils	?	5
b)	30 children are in 10 boats.	30 children	10	?
c)	Ben has 36 stickers. He gives 9 stickers to each of his friends.			
d)	Don has 12 books. He puts 3 on each shelf.			
e)	15 girls sit at 3 tables.			
f)	30 students are in 2 school buses.			
g)	9 fruit bars are shared among 3 children.			
h)	15 chairs are in 3 rows.			
i)	Each basket holds 4 eggs. There are 12 eggs altogether.			

7. Draw a picture using dots and circles to solve each part of Question 6.

8. Draw a picture using dots and circles to show the answer.

a) 15 dots; 5 sets

_____ dots in each set

b) 16 dots; 8 dots in each set

_____ sets

c) 15 dots; 5 dots in each set

_____ sets

d) 8 dots; 4 sets

_____ dots in each set

e) 10 children are in 2 boats.

How many children are in each boat? _____

f) Tasha has 12 pencils.
She puts 3 pencils in each box.

How many boxes does she have? _____

g) 4 boys share 12 marbles.

How many marbles does each boy get? _____

h) Abella has 10 apples.
She gives 2 apples to each friend.

How many friends receive apples? _____

i) 6 children go sailing in 2 boats.

How many children are in each boat? _____

j) Alex has 10 stickers.
He puts 2 on each page.

How many pages does he use? _____

Every division equation can be rewritten as an **addition equation** and a **multiplication equation**.

Example: "15 divided into sets of 3 equals 5 sets" gives

"adding 3 five times equals 15"   and   "5 groups of 3 equals 15"

3 + 3 + 3 + 3 + 3 = 15   **5 × 3 = 15**

1. Draw a picture and write addition and multiplication equations for each division equation.

   a) $8 \div 2 = 4$ b) $12 \div 6 = 2$ c) $12 \div 3 = 4$

   $2 + 2 + 2 + 2 = 8$ _____   _____

   $4 \times 2 = 8$ _____   _____

2. Draw a picture and write a division equation for each multiplication, addition, or subtraction equation.

   a) $3 \times 4 = 12$ b) $3 \times 6 = 18$

   $12 \div 4 = 3$ _____

   c) $5 + 5 + 5 + 5 = 20$ d) $2 \times 5 = 10$

   _____   _____

   e) $5 \times 3 = 15$ f) $18 - 9 - 9 = 0$

   _____   _____

You can divide by skip counting on a number line. Example: Solve the problem **15 ÷ 3 = ?**.

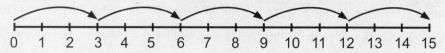

0 1 2 3 4 5 6 7 8 9 10 11 12 13 14 15

It takes 5 skips of 3 to get 15: **3 + 3 + 3 + 3 + 3 = 15**, so **15 ÷ 3 = 5**.

1. Draw a picture to show skip counting and complete the division equation.

a)

$8 \div 2 =$ _____

b)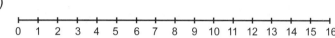

$16 \div 8 =$ _____

2. What division equation does the picture represent?

a)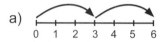

_____

b)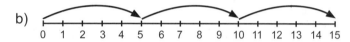

_____

You can also divide by skip counting on your fingers.

Example: To find **45 ÷ 9**, skip count by 9s until you reach 45.

The number of fingers you have up when you stop is the answer. So **45 ÷ 9 = 5**.

3. Find the answer by skip counting on your fingers.

a) $14 \div 2 =$ ___7___

b) $18 \div 3 =$ _____

c) $20 \div 5 =$ _____

d) $36 \div 6 =$ _____

e) $48 \div 8 =$ _____

f) $63 \div 7 =$ _____

4. Use your answers from Question 3 to complete the equations.
   Was each answer correct?

a) Does $2 \times \boxed{7} =$ _14_ ? ✓

b) Does $3 \times \boxed{} =$ _18_ ?

c) Does $5 \times \boxed{} =$ ____ ?

d) Does $6 \times \boxed{} =$ ____ ?

e) Does ____ $\times \boxed{} =$ ____ ?

f) Does ____ $\times \boxed{} =$ ____ ?

5. 30 students sit in 6 rows. How many students are in each row?

NS4-35 Division and Multiplication

1. Write two multiplication equations and two division equations for each picture.

a)

_____

_____

_____

_____

b)

_____

_____

_____

_____

c)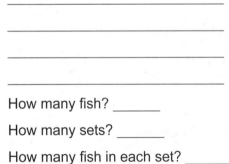

_____

_____

_____

_____

How many fish? _____

How many sets? _____

How many fish in each set? _____

d)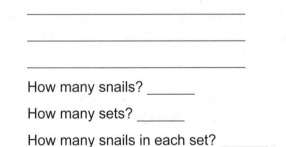

_____

_____

_____

_____

How many snails? _____

How many sets? _____

How many snails in each set? _____

2. Find the answer to the division problem by first finding the answer to the multiplication problem.

a) $4 \times \boxed{5} = 20$

$20 \div 4 = \boxed{5}$

b) $6 \times \boxed{} = 12$

$12 \div 6 = \boxed{}$

c) $5 \times \boxed{} = 20$

$20 \div 5 = \boxed{}$

d) $6 \times \boxed{} = 30$

$30 \div 6 = \boxed{}$

e) $9 \times \boxed{} = 45$

$45 \div 9 = \boxed{}$

f) $7 \times \boxed{} = 21$

$21 \div 7 = \boxed{}$

g) $3 \times \boxed{} = 24$

$24 \div 3 = \boxed{}$

h) $6 \times \boxed{} = 24$

$24 \div 6 = \boxed{}$

3. Fill in the blanks for each picture.

a) $\boxed{||||}\ \boxed{||||}\ \boxed{||||}$

_____ lines

_____ lines in each set

_____ sets

b) $\boxed{|||||}\ \boxed{|||||}\ \boxed{|||||}$

_____ lines in total

_____ sets

_____ lines in each set

c) $\boxed{||||}\ \boxed{||||}\ \boxed{||||}\ \boxed{||||}$

_____ lines in each group

_____ groups

_____ lines

d) $\boxed{||}\ \boxed{||}\ \boxed{||}\ \boxed{||}\ \boxed{||}$

_____ lines in each set

_____ sets

_____ lines altogether

e) $\boxed{||||}\ \boxed{||||}$

_____ lines

_____ lines in each set

_____ sets

f) $\boxed{|||}\ \boxed{|||}\ \boxed{|||}\ \boxed{|||}$

_____ lines in total

_____ groups

_____ lines in each group

g) $\boxed{||||||}\ \boxed{||||||}$

_____ lines

_____ lines in each set

_____ sets

h) $\boxed{||}\ \boxed{||}\ \boxed{||}$

_____ lines in total

_____ sets

_____ lines in each set

i) $\boxed{|||}\ \boxed{|||}\ \boxed{|||}$

_____ lines in each group

_____ groups

_____ lines

4. Draw a picture of …

a) 16 lines altogether; 4 lines in each set; 4 sets.   b) 8 lines; 4 lines in each set; 2 sets.

c) 6 sets; 3 lines in each set; 18 lines in total.   d) 12 lines; 2 sets; 6 lines in each set.

5. Draw a picture *and* write two division equations and two multiplication equations.

a) 20 lines; 5 sets; 4 lines in each set   b) 15 lines; 5 lines in each set; 3 sets

6. Draw a picture to find the missing piece of information.

a) __5__ lines in each set

_____ sets

__15__ lines altogether

b) __18__ lines

_____ lines in each set

__3__ sets

c) _____ lines in total

__3__ groups

__4__ lines in each group

1. Multiply or divide to find the missing information (?) in the row.

	Total number of things	Number of sets	Number in each set	Multiplication or division equation
a)	?	6	3	$6 \times 3 = 18$
b)	20	4	?	$20 \div 4 = 5$
c)	15	?	5	
d)	10	2	?	
e)	?	4	6	
f)	21	7	?	

2. Write a multiplication or division equation to solve the problem.

a) 18 things in total
3 things in each set

$\underline{\quad\quad 18 \div 3 = 6 \quad\quad}$

How many sets?

$\underline{\quad 6 \quad}$

b) 5 sets
4 things in each set

$\underline{\quad\quad\quad\quad\quad\quad\quad}$

How many things in total?

$\underline{\quad\quad\quad}$

c) 15 things in total
5 sets

$\underline{\quad\quad\quad\quad\quad\quad\quad}$

How many things in each set?

$\underline{\quad\quad\quad}$

d) 8 groups
3 things in each group

$\underline{\quad\quad\quad\quad\quad\quad\quad}$

How many things in total?

$\underline{\quad\quad\quad}$

e) 6 things in each set
12 things in total

$\underline{\quad\quad\quad\quad\quad\quad\quad}$

How many sets?

$\underline{\quad\quad\quad}$

f) 5 groups
10 things in total

$\underline{\quad\quad\quad\quad\quad\quad\quad}$

How many in each group?

$\underline{\quad\quad\quad}$

g) 5 things in each set
4 sets

$\underline{\quad\quad\quad\quad\quad\quad\quad}$

How many things in total?

$\underline{\quad\quad\quad}$

h) 4 things in each set
6 sets

$\underline{\quad\quad\quad\quad\quad\quad\quad}$

How many things in total?

$\underline{\quad\quad\quad}$

i) 16 things in total
8 sets

$\underline{\quad\quad\quad\quad\quad\quad\quad}$

How many things in each set?

$\underline{\quad\quad\quad}$

3. Fill in the table. Use a question mark to show what you don't know. Then write a multiplication or division equation in the last column and answer the question.

		Total number of things	Number of sets	Number in each set	Multiplication or division equation
a)	20 people 4 vans	20	4	?	$20 \div 4 = 5$ How many people in each van? ___5___
b)	3 marbles in each jar 6 jars				How many marbles? _____
c)	15 flowers 5 pots				How many flowers in each pot? _____
d)	4 chairs at each table 2 tables				How many chairs? _____
e)	18 pillows 6 beds				How many pillows on each bed? _____
f)	18 houses 9 houses on each block				How many blocks? _____

This is the **fact family** for the multiplication equation **3 × 5 = 15**:

$3 \times 5 = 15$	$5 \times 3 = 15$	$15 \div 3 = 5$	$15 \div 5 = 3$

4. Complete the fact family for each equation.

a) $5 \times 2 = 10$ b) $4 \times 3 = 12$ c) $12 \div 2 = 6$ d) $8 \div 4 = 2$

_____   _____   _____   _____

_____   _____   _____   _____

_____   _____   _____   _____

NS4-37 Unit Rates

> A **rate** is a comparison of two quantities in different units.
>
> In a **unit rate**, one of the quantities is equal to one. For instance, "1 apple costs 30¢" is a unit rate.

1. Fill in the missing information.

   a) 1 book costs $4.

   2 books cost _____.

   3 books cost _____.

   4 books cost _____.

   b) 1 ticket costs $5.

   2 tickets cost _____.

   3 tickets cost _____.

   4 tickets cost _____.

   c) 1 apple costs 20¢.

   2 apples cost _____.

   3 apples cost _____.

   4 apples cost _____.

   d) 20 km in 1 hour

   _____ km in 3 hours

   e) $12 allowance in 1 week

   _____ allowance in 4 weeks

   f) 1 teacher for 25 students

   3 teachers for _____ students

   g) 10 cups of water for 1 kg of rice

   _____ cups of water for 5 kg of rice

2. In the pictures below, 1 centimetre represents 3 metres. Use a ruler to find out how long each whale is.

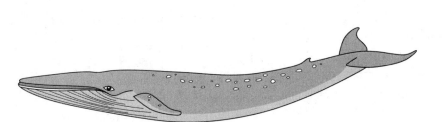

   Killer Whale:

   Length in cm: _____

   Length in m: _____

   Blue Whale:

   Length in cm: _____

   Length in m: _____

3. Kyle earns $8 an hour babysitting. How much will he earn in 4 hours? _____

4. Alice earns $10 an hour mowing lawns. How much will she earn in 8 hours? _____

5. Find the unit rate.

   a) 2 books cost $10.

   1 book costs _____.

   b) 4 mangoes cost $12.

   1 mango costs _____.

   c) 6 cans of juice cost $12.

   1 can of juice costs _____.

6. Draw 3 times as many circles as there are squares.

a) ☐ ☐ ○ ○
   ○ ○
   ○ ○

b) ☐

c) ☐ ☐ ☐

7. Write how many times as many circles as squares.

a) ☐ ☐ ○ ○
   ○ ○
   ○ ○
   ○ ○

There are _____ times as many circles as squares.

b) ☐ ☐ ☐ ○ ○ ○
   ○ ○ ○
   ○ ○ ○
   ○ ○ ○
   ○ ○ ○

There are _____ times as many circles as squares.

c) ☐ ☐ ☐ ☐ ○ ○ ○ ○
   ○ ○ ○ ○
   ○ ○ ○ ○

There are _____ times as many circles as squares.

d) ☐ ☐ ☐ ○ ○ ○
   ○ ○ ○

There are _____ times as many circles as squares.

8. Use the multiplication equation to write how many times as many one number is than the other.

a) $35 = 5 \times 7$

35 is _____ times as many as 7.

b) $40 = 5 \times 8$

40 is _____ times as many as 8.

9. Draw a picture and write a multiplication equation.

a) There are 2 circles. There are 4 times as many triangles as circles.

b) There are 2 boys. There are 3 times as many girls as boys.

c) There are 4 blue marbles. There are twice as many red marbles as blue marbles.

10. Kim has 6 books. Ronin has 3 times as many books as Kim.
How many books does Ronin have? Explain how you know.

NS4-38 Remainders

Glen wants to share 7 strawberries with 2 friends.
He sets out 3 plates, one for himself and one for each of his friends.
He puts one strawberry at a time on each plate:

There is one strawberry left over.

7 strawberries cannot be divided equally into 3 sets. Each friend gets 2 strawberries, but one is left over.

$$7 \div 3 = 2 \text{ Remainder } 1$$

1. Can 2 people share 5 strawberries equally? Show your work using dots and circles.

2. Share the dots as equally as possible among the circles. Then fill in the blanks.
   Note: In one question, the dots can be shared equally (so there's no remainder).

   a) 7 dots in 2 circles

   b) 10 dots in 3 circles

   _____ dots in each circle; _____ dot remaining   _____ dots in each circle; _____ dot remaining

   c) 10 dots in 5 circles

   d) 9 dots in 4 circles

   _____ dots in each circle; _____ dots remaining   _____ dots in each circle; _____ dot remaining

   e) 12 dots in 5 circles

   f) 13 dots in 4 circles

   _____ dots in each circle; _____ dot remaining   _____ dots in each circle; _____ dot remaining

3. Share the dots as equally as possible. Draw a picture and write a division equation.

a) 7 dots in 3 circles

b) 11 dots in 3 circles

$7 \div 3 = 2$ *Remainder 1*

c) 14 dots in 3 circles

d) 10 dots in 6 circles

e) 10 dots in 4 circles

f) 13 dots in 5 circles

4. Three friends want to share 7 cherries. How many cherries will each friend receive? How many will be left over? Show your work and write a division equation.

5. Find two different ways to share 13 granola bars into equal groups so that one is left over.

6. Fred, Avril, and Mandy have fewer than 10 oranges and more than 3 oranges. They share the oranges equally. How many oranges do they have? Is there more than one answer?

NS4-39 Dividing Using Tens Blocks

1. Divide the blocks among 2 equal groups. Then write the division equation.

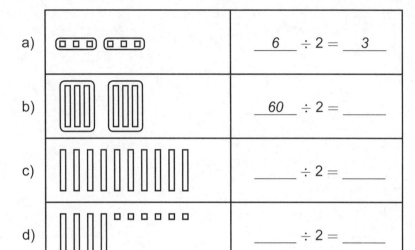

a)	$\underline{\quad 6 \quad} \div 2 = \underline{\quad 3 \quad}$
b)	$\underline{\quad 60 \quad} \div 2 = \underline{\quad\quad}$
c)	$\underline{\quad\quad} \div 2 = \underline{\quad\quad}$
d)	$\underline{\quad\quad} \div 2 = \underline{\quad\quad}$

2. a) Divide 8 tens among 4 equal groups. Then finish the division equation.

   8 tens ÷ 4 = $\underline{\quad 2 \quad}$ tens   So 80 ÷ 4 = $\underline{\quad 20 \quad}$

   b) Divide 9 tens among 3 equal groups. Then finish the division equation.

   9 tens ÷ 3 = $\underline{\quad\quad}$ tens   So 90 ÷ 3 = $\underline{\quad\quad}$

   c) Divide 6 tens among 2 equal groups. Then finish the division equation.

   6 tens ÷ 2 = $\underline{\quad\quad}$ tens   So $\underline{\quad\quad\quad}$ ÷ 2 = $\underline{\quad\quad\quad}$

3. Divide.

   a) 9 ÷ 3 = $\underline{\quad\quad}$ b) 20 ÷ 4 = $\underline{\quad\quad}$ c) 90 ÷ 3 = $\underline{\quad\quad}$ d) 40 ÷ 4 = $\underline{\quad\quad}$

   e) 99 ÷ 3 = $\underline{\quad\quad}$ f) 48 ÷ 4 = $\underline{\quad\quad}$ g) 69 ÷ 3 = $\underline{\quad\quad}$ h) 84 ÷ 4 = $\underline{\quad\quad}$

4. Draw blocks to divide.

   a) 30 ÷ 2 = $\underline{\quad\quad}$ b) 56 ÷ 2 = $\underline{\quad\quad}$

   c) 42 ÷ 3 = $\underline{\quad\quad}$ d) 15 ÷ 3 = $\underline{\quad\quad}$

1. Divide by 10.

   a) $30 \div 10 =$ _____

   b) $50 \div 10 =$ _____

   c) $80 \div 10 =$ _____

   d) $90 \div 10 =$ _____

   e) $40 \div 10 =$ _____

   f) $100 \div 10 =$ _____

   g) $70 \div 10 =$ _____

   h) $10 \div 10 =$ _____

Grace wants to calculate $60 \div 5$. She notices that there are 2 groups of 5 in every tens block. She draws 6 tens blocks then skip counts by 2 to divide.

2 4 6 8 10 12

---

2. Draw tens blocks. Then skip count by 2 to divide by 5.

   a) $30 \div 5 =$ _____

   b) $50 \div 5 =$ _____

   c) $70 \div 5 =$ _____

   d) $90 \div 5 =$ _____

   e) $20 \div 5 =$ _____

   f) $40 \div 5 =$ _____

   g) $60 \div 5 =$ _____

   h) $10 \div 5 =$ _____

Lewis notices that there are 5 groups of 2 in every ten. He calculates $40 \div 2$ by multiplying 4×5.

---

3. Divide by 2.

   a) $90 \div 2 =$ _____

   b) $60 \div 2 =$ _____

   c) $80 \div 2 =$ _____

   d) $20 \div 2 =$ _____

   e) $30 \div 2 =$ _____

   f) $10 \div 2 =$ _____

   g) $70 \div 2 =$ _____

   h) $50 \div 2 =$ _____

4. Divide by 4.

    a) $40 \div 4 =$ _____   b) $80 \div 4 =$ _____   c) $20 \div 4 =$ _____   d) $60 \div 4 =$ _____

5. Divide.

    a) $30 \div 5 =$ _____   b) $60 \div 10 =$ _____   c) $70 \div 2 =$ _____

    d) $80 \div 4 =$ _____   e) $40 \div 10 =$ _____   f) $40 \div 2 =$ _____

    g) $40 \div 5 =$ _____   h) $30 \div 3 =$ _____   i) $30 \div 2 =$ _____

    j) $30 \div 10 =$ _____   k) $70 \div 5 =$ _____   l) $90 \div 3 =$ _____

    m) $40 \div 4 =$ _____   n) $60 \div 4 =$ _____   o) $60 \div 3 =$ _____

    p) $10 \div 5 =$ _____   q) $20 \div 5 =$ _____   r) $100 \div 5 =$ _____

    s) $70 \div 10 =$ _____   t) $90 \div 5 =$ _____   u) $80 \div 5 =$ _____

    v) $100 \div 2 =$ _____   w) $50 \div 2 =$ _____   x) $20 \div 10 =$ _____

6. Divide.

    a) $30 \div 3 =$ _____   b) $90 \div 9 =$ _____   c) $80 \div 8 =$ _____

    d) $20 \div 2 =$ _____   e) $60 \div 6 =$ _____   f) $100 \div 10 =$ _____

    g) $70 \div 7 =$ _____   h) $10 \div 1 =$ _____

7. Divide by 5.

    a) $30 \div 5 =$ _____   b) $35 \div 5 =$ _____   c) $70 \div 5 =$ _____

    d) $75 \div 5 =$ _____   e) $25 \div 5 =$ _____   f) $45 \div 5 =$ _____

    g) $65 \div 5 =$ _____   h) $15 \div 5 =$ _____   i) $85 \div 5 =$ _____

    j) $55 \div 5 =$ _____   k) $95 \div 5 =$ _____   l) $5 \div 5 =$ _____

BONUS ▶ Divide by 2.

    a) $44 \div 2 =$ _____   b) $64 \div 2 =$ _____   c) $86 \div 2 =$ _____

    d) $28 \div 2 =$ _____   e) $84 \div 2 =$ _____   f) $22 \div 2 =$ _____

    g) $66 \div 2 =$ _____   h) $46 \div 2 =$ _____

To find 86 ÷ 2, divide the tens and ones separately.

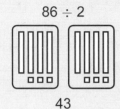

86 ÷ 2	=	80 ÷ 2	+	6 ÷ 2

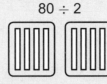

43	=	40	+	3

1. Divide one place value at a time.

   a) 64 ÷ 2 = (60 ÷ 2) + (4 ÷ 2)

      = __30__ + __2__

      = __32__

   b) 69 ÷ 3 = (60 ÷ 3) + (9 ÷ 3)

      = _____ + _____

      = _____

   c) 86 ÷ 2 = (80 ÷ 2) + (6 ÷ 2)

      = _____ + _____

      = _____

   d) 96 ÷ 3 = (_____ ÷ 3) + (_____ ÷ 3)

      = _____ + _____

      = _____

   e) 39 ÷ 3 = (____ ÷ ____) + (____ ÷ ____)

      = _____ + _____

      = _____

   f) 84 ÷ 4 = (____ ÷ ____) + (____ ÷ ____)

      = _____ + _____

      = _____

   g) 58 ÷ 2 = (____ ÷ ____) + (____ ÷ ____)

      = _____ + _____

      = _____

   h) 65 ÷ 5 = (____ ÷ ____) + (____ ÷ ____)

      = _____ + _____

      = _____

BONUS ▶ 824 ÷ 2 = (800 ÷ 2) + (20 ÷ 2) + (4 ÷ 2)

2. Check your answer to Question 1, parts a) and b) by multiplication.

   a)
   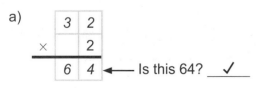
   ◀— Is this 64? ✓ _____

   b)
   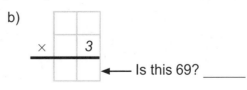
   ◀— Is this 69? _____

A rectangle with 4 squares down and
6 squares across has 24 squares in total.

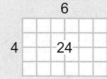

$4 \times 6 = 24$ so $24 \div 4 = 6$

3. How many squares across is the rectangle?

a) $12 \div 3 =$ _____

b)  $15 \div 3 =$ _____

4. Draw the rectangle to make the total number of squares. How many
   squares across do you need?

a)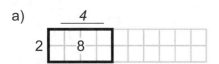

b)
$$2 \mid 14$$

5. Decide how many squares across you need to make the rectangle. Then write
   the division equation.

a)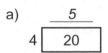

$$\underline{\quad 20 \div 4 = 5 \quad}$$

b)
$$4 \mid 40$$

_____

c)
$$4 \mid 24$$

_____

d)
$$4 \mid 36$$

_____

Tina finds $36 \div 2$ by splitting 36 into tens and ones.

$$36 = 30 + 6 \text{ so}$$
$$36 \div 2 = 15 + 3 = 18$$

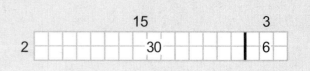

6. Use Tina's method to divide.

a) $92 \div 2$

$$\underline{\quad 45 \quad} + \underline{\quad 1 \quad}$$
$$2 \mid 90 \mid 2$$

$92 \div 2 = \underline{\quad 46 \quad}$

b) $56 \div 2$

$$\underline{\quad\quad} + \underline{\quad\quad}$$
$$2 \mid 50 \mid 6$$

$56 \div 2 =$ _____

c) $62 \div 2$

$$\underline{\quad\quad} + \underline{\quad\quad}$$
$$2 \mid \quad\quad\quad\quad \mid$$

$62 \div 2 =$ _____

d) $74 \div 2$

$$\underline{\quad\quad} + \underline{\quad\quad}$$
$$2 \mid \quad\quad\quad\quad \mid$$

$74 \div 2 =$ _____

Raj uses Tina's method to divide 78 ÷ 2, but…

… he chooses the tens and ones so that the **number of tens** is a multiple of the **number that he is dividing by**.

He uses the largest number of tens he can.

78 = 7 tens + 8 ones

= **6** tens + 18 ones

6 is a multiple of **2**

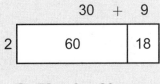

So 78 ÷ 2 = 39

7. Use Raj's method to divide.

a) 94 ÷ 2

94 = 9 tens + 4 ones

= 8 tens + _____ ones

8 is a multiple of 2

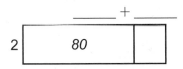

94 ÷ 2 = _____

b) 84 ÷ 3

84 = 8 tens + 4 ones

= 6 tens + _____ ones

6 is a multiple of 3

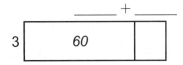

84 ÷ 3 = _____

c) 58 ÷ 2

58 ÷ 2 = _____

d) 51 ÷ 3

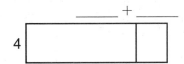

51 ÷ 3 = _____

e) 72 ÷ 3

72 ÷ 3 = _____

f) 96 ÷ 4

96 ÷ 4 = _____

8. A rectangular patio floor is covered with 84 tiles in 6 rows. How many tiles are in each row?

So there are _____ tiles in each row.

NS4-42 Estimating Quotients

1. Write **more** or **less**.

   a) 72 ÷ 8 is _____ than 80 ÷ 8

   b) 63 ÷ 3 is _____ than 60 ÷ 3

   c) 84 ÷ 7 is _____ than 70 ÷ 7

   d) 95 ÷ 5 is _____ than 100 ÷ 5

2. Replace the dividend with the next multiple of 10 to make the division easier.

   a) 76 ÷ 2 < __80__ ÷ 2

      76 ÷ 2 < __40__

   b) 56 ÷ 4 < _____ ÷ 4

      56 ÷ 4 < _____

   c) 87 ÷ 3 < _____ ÷ 3

      87 ÷ 3 < _____

   d) 98 ÷ 2 < _____ ÷ 2

      98 ÷ 2 < _____

   e) 84 ÷ 6 < _____ ÷ 6

      84 ÷ 6 < _____

   f) 52 ÷ 3 < _____ ÷ 3

      52 ÷ 3 < _____

3. Replace the dividend with the next smaller multiple of 10 to make the division easier.

   a) 66 ÷ 2 > __60__ ÷ 2

      66 ÷ 2 > __30__

   b) 66 ÷ 3 > _____ ÷ 3

      66 ÷ 3 > _____

   c) 36 ÷ 6 > _____ ÷ 6

      36 ÷ 6 > _____

   d) 88 ÷ 4 > _____ ÷ 4

      88 ÷ 4 > _____

   e) 77 ÷ 7 > _____ ÷ 7

      77 ÷ 7 > _____

   f) 99 ÷ 9 > _____ ÷ 9

      99 ÷ 9 > _____

4. Write two divisions using greater multiples of 10. Choose the division that is easiest.

   a) 45 ÷ 3 < __50__ ÷ 3 < __60__ ÷ 3

      45 ÷ 3 < __60__ ÷ 3

      45 ÷ 3 < __20__

   b) 56 ÷ 4 < _____ ÷ 4 < _____ ÷ 4

      56 ÷ 4 < _____ ÷ 4

      56 ÷ 4 < _____

   c) 56 ÷ 7 < _____ ÷ 7 < _____ ÷ 7

      56 ÷ 7 < _____ ÷ 7

      56 ÷ 7 < _____

   d) 54 ÷ 6 < _____ ÷ 6 < _____ ÷ 6

      54 ÷ 6 < _____ ÷ 6

      54 ÷ 6 < _____

5. Write two divisions using smaller multiples of 10. Choose the division that is easiest.

a) $45 \div 3 > \underline{40} \div 3 > \underline{30} \div 3$

    $45 \div 3 > \underline{30} \div 3$

    $45 \div 3 > \underline{10}$

b) $56 \div 4 > \underline{} \div 4 > \underline{} \div 4$

    $56 \div 4 > \underline{} \div 4$

    $56 \div 4 > \underline{}$

c) $47 \div 3 > \underline{} \div 3 > \underline{} \div 3$

    $47 \div 3 > \underline{} \div 3$

    $47 \div 3 > \underline{}$

d) $72 \div 6 > \underline{} \div 6 > \underline{} \div 6$

    $72 \div 6 > \underline{} \div 6$

    $72 \div 6 > \underline{}$

6. Use your answers to Questions 4 and 5 to find what the division is between.

a) $45 \div 3$ is between $\underline{10}$ and $\underline{20}$.

b) $56 \div 4$ is between $\underline{}$ and $\underline{}$.

7. Choose a multiple of 10 that makes the division easier. Is the quotient greater or smaller? Write the sign in the circle. Then calculate the answer.

a) $45 \div 5 \;\boxed{<}\; \underline{50} \div 5 = \underline{}$

b) $84 \div 7 \;\bigcirc\; \underline{} \div 7 = \underline{}$

c) $72 \div 4 \;\bigcirc\; \underline{} \div 4 = \underline{}$

d) $72 \div 6 \;\bigcirc\; \underline{} \div 6 = \underline{}$

8. Estimate then calculate the answer.

a) 6 cars lined up make a line 24 m long. How long is each car?

b) 7 batteries weigh 84 grams. How much does each battery weigh?

9. Clara says that $72 \div 3$ is more than 20. Ray says it is less than 30. Who is correct? Explain.

Ivan is preparing snacks for 4 classes. He needs to divide 95 apples into 4 groups.
He uses long division and a model to solve the problem.

Step 1: Write the numbers like this:

the number of groups ⟶ 4⟌95 ⟵ the number of objects
to divide into groups

$95 = 9$ tens $+ 5$ ones

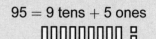

1. Fill in the blanks for the division statement.

a) 2⟌53

_____ groups

_____ tens

_____ ones

b) 5⟌71

_____ groups

_____ tens

_____ ones

c) 4⟌97

_____ groups

_____ tens

_____ ones

d) 5⟌88

_____ groups

_____ tens

_____ ones

Step 2: How many tens can be put in each group?

2 tens in each group ⟶ **2**

4 groups ⟶ 4⟌ 9 | 5

2. For each division problem, write how many groups have been made and how many
tens are in each group.

a) 4⟌ 5 | 5

_____ groups

_____ ten in
each group

b) 5⟌ 9 | 7

_____ groups

_____ ten in
each group

c) 3⟌ 7 | 6

_____ groups

_____ tens in
each group

d) 3⟌ 8 | 9

_____ groups

_____ tens in
each group

3. How many tens can be put in each group?

a) 4⟌ 8 | 7 → **2**

b) 3⟌ 9 | 4

c) 6⟌ 7 | 4

d) 2⟌ 9 | 8

e) 2⟌ 8 | 5

f) 3⟌ 6 | 7

g) 8⟌ 9 | 1

h) 3⟌ 8 | 2

Step 3: How many tens have been placed into groups altogether?

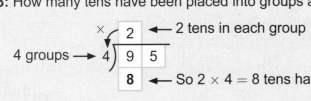

$2 \times 4 = 8$

4 groups ⟶ 4) 9 5   × 2 ← 2 tens in each group

8 ← So $2 \times 4 = 8$ tens have been placed

---

4. Multiply to decide how many tens have been placed.

a)

```
   × ⌐ 2
3 ) 8  7
    6
```

b)

```
     2
4 ) 9  9
```

c)

```
     3
2 ) 7  9
```

d)

```
     4
2 ) 8  9
```

5. Multiply to decide how many tens have been placed. Then answer the questions.

a)

```
     2
3 ) 8  7
```

How many groups? _____

How many tens? _____

How many tens in each group? _____

How many tens placed altogether? _____

b)

```
     2
4 ) 9  6
```

How many groups? _____

How many tens? _____

How many tens in each group? _____

How many tens placed altogether? _____

6. Skip count to find out how many tens can be placed in each group. Then multiply to find out how many tens have been placed.

a)

```
8 ) 9  4
```

b)

```
5 ) 9  4
```

c)

```
2 ) 8  8
```

d)

```
7 ) 9  5
```

e)

```
4 ) 8  5
```

f)

```
4 ) 9  2
```

g)

```
5 ) 6  3
```

h)

```
2 ) 9  8
```

Step 4: How many tens are left over?

There are 9 tens.
Ivan has placed 8. ———————→

$9 - 8 = 1$ ten is left over ———→

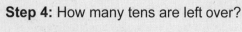

9 − 8 = 1 ten left over

7. Carry out the first four steps of long division.

a)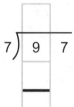

b)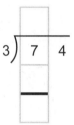

c)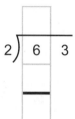

d)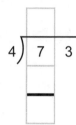

e)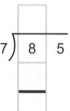

f)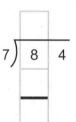

g)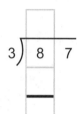

h)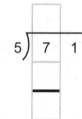

Step 5: There are 1 ten and 5 ones left over.
So there are 15 ones left over.

Write 5 beside the 1 to show this.

←—— There are 15 ones still to place ——↗

8. Carry out the first five steps of long division.

a)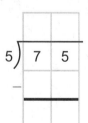

b)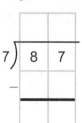

c)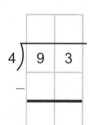

d)

e)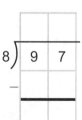

f)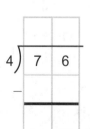

g)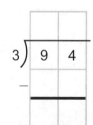

h)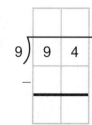

Step 6: How many of the 15 ones can be placed in each group?

Divide to find out.

   ← 15 ÷ 4 = 3 R ?

How many ones are left over? _____

9. Carry out the first six steps of long division.

a)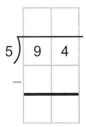

b)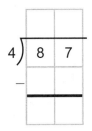

c)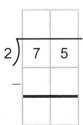

d)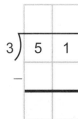

e)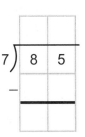

f)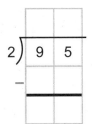

g)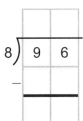

h)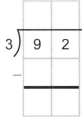

Step 7: How many ones are left over?

— 3 ones in each group and 4 groups

— 4 × 3 = 12 ones were placed

— 15 − 12 = 3 ones are left over

left over

95 ÷ 4 = 23 with 3 left over

10. Carry out all seven steps of long division.

a)

b)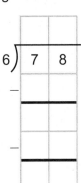

c)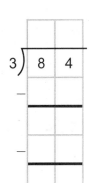

d)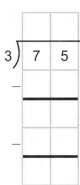

11. a) How many weeks are there in 84 days?

  b) A boat can hold 4 children. How many boats will 72 children need?

1. Tom needs new tires for his car. Each tire costs $263. How much do all 4 tires cost?

2. Jennifer plants 84 lilies in 4 flower beds. How many lilies are in each flower bed?

3. A square garden needs 68 m of fencing altogether. How long is each side of the garden?

4. John paid $72 for 6 T-shirts. How much did each T-shirt cost?

5. How many weeks are there in the month of February?

6. Armand buys 3 pens for $11. Then he buys 5 more pens for $13. How much did he end up paying per pen?

7. A queen ant can lay one egg every ten seconds. How many eggs can she lay in …

   a) 1 minute?   b) 2 minutes?   c) an hour?

8. 92 students attend a play on 4 buses. There are an equal number of students on each bus.

   a) How many students are on each bus?

   b) A ticket for the play costs $6. How much will it cost for one busload of students to attend the play?

9. Find two different ways to share 14 apples in equal groups so there are 2 apples left over.

10. Find three numbers that give the same remainder when divided by 3.

11. A robin lays *at least* 3 eggs and *no more than* 6 eggs.

    a) What is the least number of eggs 3 robins' nests would hold (if there were eggs laid in each nest)?

    b) What is the greatest number of eggs 3 robins' nests would hold?

    c) Three robins' nests contain 13 eggs. Draw a picture to show 2 ways the eggs could be shared among the nests.

12. Aputik used 3 times as many blue beads as red beads for a bracelet. She used 12 more blue beads than yellow beads. She used 3 yellow beads.

   a) How many beads of each color did Aputik use?

   b) How many beads did she use in total?

13. Snow geese can fly 200 km in 3 hours. They can fly for a very long time.

   a) How far can they travel in 6 hours? 9 hours?

   b) Some snow geese flew for 18 hours, rested, and then flew for another 21 hours. How long did the geese travel? How far did the geese travel?

14. A narwhal is an arctic whale. The adult male has one very long tooth. An adult narwhal is about 5 m long from nose to tail, and its tooth is 3 m long. Use the diagram to tell how long a baby narwhal is.

adult male narwhal

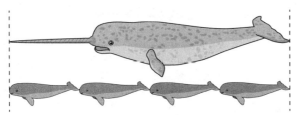

baby narwhal

15. An eraser is 5 cm long. A pencil is 15 cm long. Write your answer to the question as a full sentence.

   a) How many times longer is the pencil than the eraser?

   b) How many centimetres longer is the pencil than the eraser?

16. An elephant weighs 2000 kg and is 2 m tall. Is this elephant 1000 times heavier than it is tall? Explain.

17. There are 5 people at a pizza party. They ordered 2 pizzas. Each pizza has 8 slices. Each person gets the same number of slices. How many slices can each person have?

18. There are 52 avocados in a crate. Thirteen are spoiled. Nora packs the rest into bags of 5 avocados. How many bags can she make?

19. There are 24 students in one class and 23 students in another class going on a field trip. Each car can hold 4 students. How many cars are needed to transport all the students?